4:50 2/24

SCIENCE FACTS

WEATHER

A rainbow reveals the colors of sunlight.

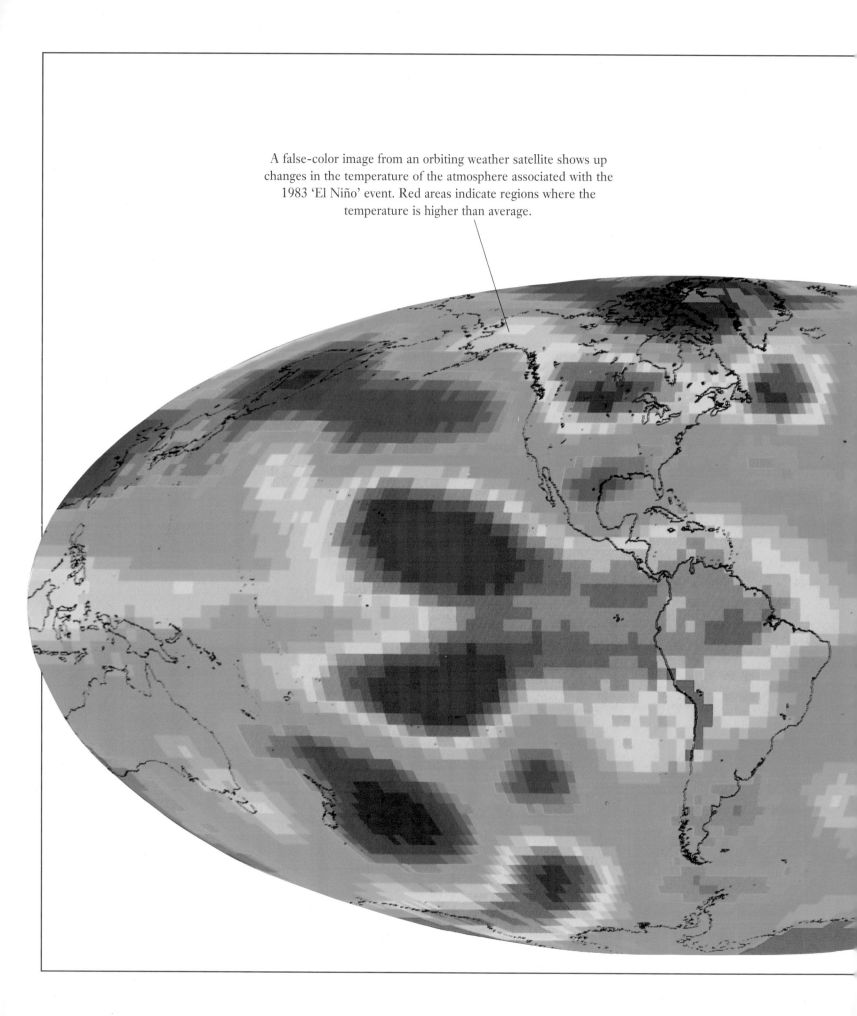

A false-color image from an orbiting weather satellite shows up changes in the temperature of the atmosphere associated with the 1983 'El Niño' event. Red areas indicate regions where the temperature is higher than average.

SCIENCE FACTS

WEATHER

PETER LAFFERTY

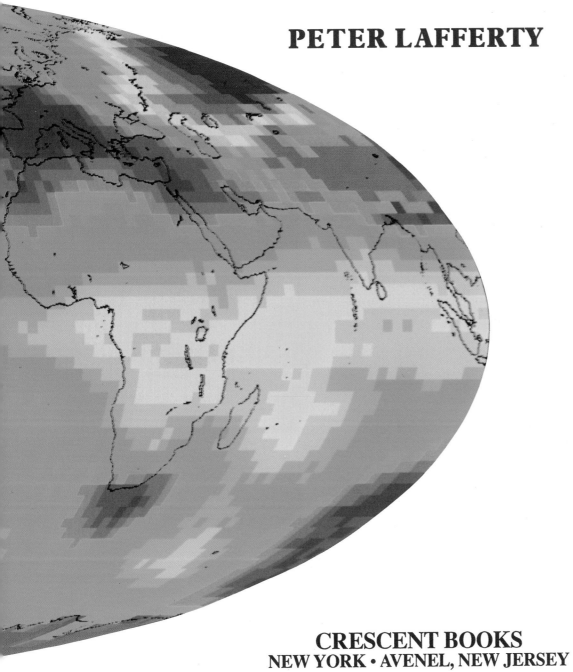

CRESCENT BOOKS
NEW YORK • AVENEL, NEW JERSEY

CLB 2835

© 1992 Colour Library Books Ltd., Godalming, Surrey, England.

This 1992 edition published by Crescent Books,
distributed by Outlet Book Company, Inc.,
a Random House Company
40 Engelhard Avenue, Avenel, New Jersey 07001

Printed and bound in Italy

ISBN 0 517 06557 6

8 7 6 5 4 3 2 1

The Author
Peter Lafferty is a fulltime author who specializes in science writing,
particularly with a younger audience in mind. His particular areas of interest
are astronomy, physics and chemistry, technology, computing, and the history
of science. He has written more than 35 books and has contributed to many
major encyclopedias.

Credits
Editor: Philip de Ste. Croix
Designers: Stonecastle Graphics Ltd.
Color artwork: Rod Ferring © Colour Library Books Ltd.
Picture Editor: Miriam Sharland
Production: Ruth Arthur, Sally Connolly, Andrew Whitelaw
Director of Production: Gerald Hughes
Typesetting: SX Composing Ltd.
Printed and bound by New Interlitho SpA, Italy

This is how the Earth looks to a
weather satellite in geostationary
orbit. Here we see Australia,
Asia, and the Pacific Ocean.
Cloud systems appear in yellow.

CONTENTS

Weather lore

Weather watching must have been one of the earliest pastimes. Over the centuries, rules, sayings, and rhymes about the weather have been passed down from father to son, and mother to daughter. Weather lore – the ancient rules and prediction methods – is a good place to start any study of the weather.

Whether it's cold or whether it's hot
We shall have weather, whether or not.

No doubt about that one! But are all weather rhymes and rules true? One true rule is

Rain before seven
Fine before eleven

This is generally accurate because rain belts usually last about four hours. Another reliable rhyme is

The Moon and the weather
May change together,
But a change of the Moon
Does not change the weather.

The appearance of the Moon is a useful aid to

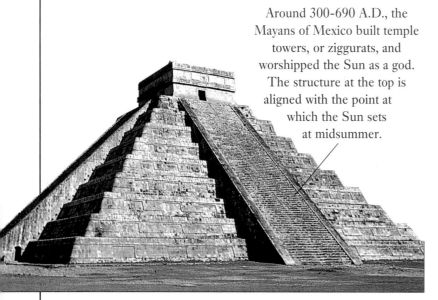

Around 300-690 A.D., the Mayans of Mexico built temple towers, or ziggurats, and worshipped the Sun as a god. The structure at the top is aligned with the point at which the Sun sets at midsummer.

predicting rain: ice crystals in rain clouds produce a ring or halo around the Moon. A sharply-outlined Moon indicates the possibility of frost, since the absence of clouds allows heat to flow quickly from the ground during the night.

There are numerous rhymes and sayings about the winds.

The north wind doth blow
And we shall have snow.

When the wind is in the east,
'tis neither good for man nor beast.

The wind in the west suits everyone best.

Unfortunately, most sayings about winds have to be

Stonehenge, on the Salisbury Plain in southern England, may have been used as an annual calendar. On midsummer morning the Sun rises over the top of the Heel Stone.

Some plants close their flowers when the air becomes damp. The petals of morning glory close when damp air is present and so indicate the approach of rain.

Seaweed is a reliable natural indicator that rain is on the way. Moisture in the air makes it damp and slimy.

Larch cones open when the weather is fine. When the cones are tightly closed, rain is on the way.

treated carefully. They may only be true in particular places or areas. For instance, the cold winds come from the south in the southern hemisphere, so the north wind could never bring snow as the rhyme says. In the northern hemisphere, the rhyme is more useful.

Sky color or appearance is often used to predict weather.

Red sky at night, shepherds' delight;
Red sky at morning, shepherds' warning.

Alas, as all shepherds know, there are different kinds of red sky, and the type of cloud is a better indicator of coming weather than sky color. An evening sky of soft, pale red, with few clouds, does probably indicate a fine day tomorrow. However, an intense red sky with heavy clouds at night means rain. Once again, the lesson is that, although weather rhymes are interesting to hear and collect, it is better to rely on science for accurate forecasts.

Our changing weather

Is our weather getting worse? In recent years, huge storms, devastating hurricanes, widespread floods, and prolonged droughts have made headlines around the world. In Africa, the Sahel – a wide belt of land south of the Sahara that stretches from Senegal in the west to Sudan in the east – has had little rain since 1968. The natural grassland of the area has been reduced to a barren dusty wasteland. Famine threatened over 35 million people in the Sahel during the mid-1980s. In Ethiopia, the northern areas of Tigre and Eritrea suffered from similar droughts and famine. In Europe, 1990 was a drought year. The water shortage in Greece was the worst for 50 years. It was so hot in Britain that road surfaces melted. North America experienced a major drought in the 1980s. In 1988, the Midwest was as dry as in the 1930s when the 'Dust Bowl' conditions turned fields to dust.

At other times, too much water was the problem. Exceptional floods occurred in the semi-arid areas of eastern Australia in 1988, 1989, and 1990. In July 1991, two of China's biggest cities were threatened by the country's worst floods in 100 years. The cities of Nanjing and Shanghai were in danger as the waters of the Chang (Yangtze) river rose amid continuous torrential rain. More than 1,700 people were killed; 2 million were left homeless. At the same time, typhoon *Zeke* hit the southern provinces.

In October 1987, a huge storm hit the southern areas of England and adjacent areas of Europe. It was the worst storm in the region since 1703, with wind gusts reaching speeds of 108mph (174km/h). The damage in some city centers, such as Brighton on the south coast of England, resembled the effects of a bombing raid. In January and February 1990 freak weather produced more great storms across Britain and Europe.

Photographs taken from space provide a complete picture of the world's weather. A storm can be tracked right round the globe.

These meteorologists are setting up apparatus to take measurements of temperature, moisture, and wind speed.

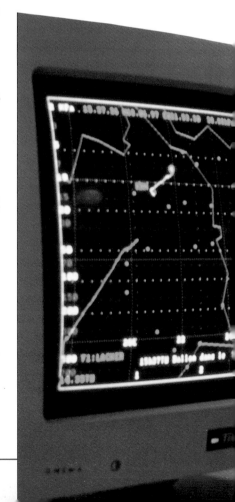

Freak weather conditions seem to be becoming more common. Unusually cold winters have hit the eastern half of the U.S. in 9 of the last 15 years. Is the world's weather and climate changing? Many people – including some scientists – think the world is gradually becoming warmer as the result of air pollution. This global warming is thought to be responsible for the freak weather of recent years. Other scientists are not so sure. Perhaps the world's climate and weather is more variable than expected. Perhaps we have become too accustomed to the 'good' weather that was common in the early part of this century. We are surprised when the weather reverts to its normal uncertain, and violent, behavior.

Severe droughts during the 1980s have threatened millions of people in Africa with starvation. The Namib Desert on the west coast of South Africa is an area that receives little rain even in good years.

A hurricane can cause enormous damage. This one in Palm Beach, Florida, had winds of up to 125mph (200km/h). There is now an early warning system to warn if hurricanes are likely.

Scientists studying the upper atmosphere use balloons to take measurements and carry out experiments. The flight paths of a balloon are here plotted on a computer.

The weather machine

Science tells us that the weather is a giant machine – the weather machine. It is by looking at the parts of the weather machine, seeing how they work, and how they fit together, that we can understand the constantly changing weather that we see outside our window.

Like all machines, the weather machine is powered by energy. Perhaps the first thing that is obvious from the pounding rain, stormy winds, and loud thunderclaps, is that they are full of violent energy. This energy comes from the Sun, the ultimate source of almost all energy on Earth. The Sun's energy reaches the Earth as radiation – light, heat, and other more energetic forms, such as ultraviolet rays.

The radiation falls on, and travels through, the atmosphere. The ground is heated by the Sun's radiation and, in turn, the air above the ground is also heated. The heated air rises, carrying some heat away from the ground. Or perhaps, the radiation falls on a lake, sea, or pool of water. If the water becomes hot enough, it evaporates. Water vapor rises into the air, once again carrying heat upward. We begin to see a complex interaction of the parts of the weather machine – energy, air, water.

The weather machine acts rather like a refrigerator, air conditioner, or heat pump. In all these machines, heat is carried from one place to

The beauty of winter. A dim Sun illuminates frost on the trees, but does not melt it.

Heat rays, also called infrared radiation, are given out by all objects. This house is giving out most heat from the orange and white areas, and least from the green areas.

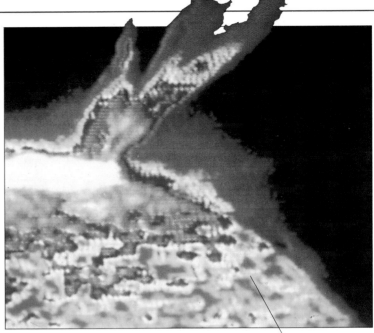

Lightning strikes at sunset, photographed over Tucson, Arizona. Lightning is really a giant electric spark, like that which can jump from your comb when you tidy your hair.

A giant flame, called a prominence, erupting thousands of miles into space from the Sun, recorded using an ultraviolet camera aboard the Skylab spacecraft in 1973.

another by a liquid or gas. In the weather machine, water-laden air blown by the winds carries the heat from hot places to colder places. This is a vitally necessary task because the Sun's energy does not fall equally on all parts of the Earth; the Sun's energy is more concentrated in the tropics than at the poles. At any given moment, the temperature difference between the Arctic and the tropics may be as much as 180°F (82°C). Weather is Nature's way of evening out this unequal heat distribution.

Of course, the weather machine is much more complicated than a refrigerator. The spinning of the Earth bends winds so that they flow in unexpected directions. Mountain ranges deflect the winds, forcing them upward to release their load of water vapor prematurely as rain. Oceans, lakes, rivers, deserts, and icecaps, also have their effect. Immense storms – hurricanes and tornadoes – disrupt the normal air flows. And human activity can affect the working of the weather machine.

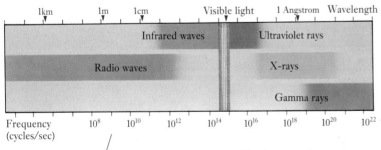

The electromagnetic spectrum. Energy from the Sun reaches the Earth as electromagnetic waves – ripples of electricity and magnetism traveling through

space. Each type of wave has a different wavelength (distance between wave crests) and frequency (number of waves each second).

The Sun – fireball in the sky

The Sun is a fiery ball of hot gases whose seething outer layer has a temperature of 11,000°F (6,000°C). Deep inside the Sun, it is even hotter – 27 million °F (15 million °C). At this enormous temperature, hydrogen – the main material in the Sun – is converted into helium, and energy is produced by a process called nuclear fusion. A hydrogen bomb produces its energy in the same way as the Sun, but is far less powerful. The energy produced by the Sun pours out into the darkness of space as radiation – mainly light and heat. Because it is pouring out energy, the Sun is losing weight all the time – at a rate of 4.5 million tons (4 million tonnes) each second. Even so, it is large enough to shine for another 5 billion years. About 93 million miles (150 million km) away, some of the Sun's radiation reaches a small planet – our home, Earth. Only about one two-billionths of the Sun's radiation is intercepted by the Earth. Although we only receive a small fraction of the Sun's energy, what we do get is enough to make life possible, and to drive the global weather machine.

The Sun's diameter is 865,000 miles (1,392,000km). It is 1,300,000 times larger than the Earth.

Nuclear fusion in the laboratory. The blue haze inside this fusion device is heated hydrogen, similar to that inside the Sun.

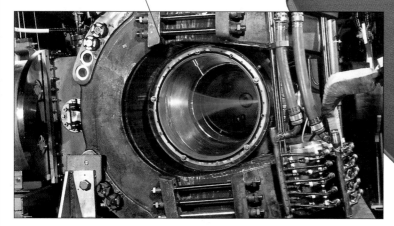

Giant flames called prominences shoot out from the Sun's surface up to a distance of 300,000 miles (500,000km).

Fusion takes place in the central core of the Sun. The energy that is produced can take 10 million years to reach the surface.

In 1905, Albert Einstein showed that a small amount of matter could be changed into a vast amount of energy.

This ultraviolet image taken in 1973 from the Skylab space station shows the turbulent energy of the Sun.

❏ If the Earth was the size and weight of a table tennis ball, the Sun would measure 12ft (3.8m) across and weigh 3 tons (2.7 tonnes). On this scale, the Earth would orbit the Sun at a distance of 1,325ft (403m).

❏ Light takes one-tenth of a second to travel from New York to London, 8 minutes to reach the Earth from the Sun, and 4.3 years to reach Earth from the nearest star.

❏ The weight of the Sun is 2 billion billion billion tons (1.8 billion billion billion tonnes), about 333,420 times that of the Earth.

❏ An area of the Sun's surface the size of a postage stamp (one square inch or 6.25cm^2) shines with the power of 1,500,000 candles.

❏ If a pin was heated to the same temperature as the center of the Sun, its heat would set alight everything within 60 miles (100km) of it.

❏ All the coal, oil, gas, and wood on Earth would only keep the Sun burning for a few days.

❏ The Sun produces more energy every minute than all the energy used on Earth in a whole year.

❏ Because it is pouring energy out into space so rapidly, the Sun is losing a weight equivalent to a million elephants every second.

Air – the Earth's warm blanket

The Earth is covered in a warm blanket of air – the atmosphere. The atmosphere keeps our planet at a comfortable temperature because it lets heat from the Sun penetrate through to the ground, but stops outgoing heat escaping into space. Without the atmosphere, temperatures on Earth would rise to 180°F (82°C) during the day, and drop to −220°F (−140°C) below zero at night. Air is a mixture of gases. Dry air is made up mainly of 78 percent nitrogen, 21 percent oxygen, 0.9 percent argon, with other gases, such as neon, helium, methane, krypton, and hydrogen, making up less than 0.002 percent. Carbon dioxide, one of the 'greenhouse gases' that keep heat in, makes up only about 0.03 percent. Of course, air is rarely dry; most air contains water vapor, a vital ingredient of weather. The layer of air around the Earth has weight. The air thus exerts a pressure as it weighs down on people and things below it. At sea level, the atmosphere exerts an average pressure of about 14.7 pounds per square inch (101 kilopascals). Meteorologists measure pressure in units called millibars; 1 millibar equals 0.0145 pounds per square inch. So, the average sea level air pressure is 1,013 millibars.

The atmosphere gets thinner higher up. At a height of 18,000ft (5,500m) pressure is half that at sea level. Climbers need extra oxygen to help them breathe.

When air is heated, it expands and rises. This balloon flies because the hot air inside makes it less dense than the air around it.

This satellite map shows the 'hole' in the ozone layer at a height of 20-30 miles (32-48km) over Antarctica on October 3, 1990. It appears here as the pink, purple, and black areas. The scale of colors represents Dobson units, which are a measurement of ozone in the atmosphere.

525

325

DU

125

The hole in the ozone layer may be caused by chemicals called chlorofluorocarbons (CFCs) used in aerosols and refrigerators. It was first observed in 1980.

The atmosphere is arranged in layers. The troposphere is where the weather develops. At the top of the stratosphere is the ozone layer, which protects us from harmful ultraviolet rays from the Sun. Above the ozone layer are the mesosphere and thermosphere which merges into space.

Height
(ft × 1,000)

THERMOSPHERE

300 —

250 —

MESOSPHERE

200 —

150 —

STRATOSPHERE

100 —

50 —

TROPOSPHERE

Temperature   −80   −40   0   32   60
(°F)

The energetic atmosphere

A steam engine converts heat energy into movement, or kinetic energy. The hot, energy-filled steam is released inside the engine and rushes into the cylinders, driving the pistons that in turn cause the wheels to move. A similar energy conversion drives the weather machine. Energy arrives at the Earth in the form of radiation. Some of this radiation is absorbed by the atmosphere; some is reflected back into space by clouds. About half the radiation reaches the ground where it is absorbed. The ground, warmed by the Sun's energy, in turn heats the air above it. Where the Sun's heat is most intense, updrafts of air are created as the hot air rises. These updrafts may be small local breezes, or large-scale global winds that howl across continents. They carry water vapor drawn up from lakes and oceans by the Sun's heat. When the vapor cools in the upper atmosphere, rain falls. So, the vast, churning movements of the atmosphere that produce our weather are created by the Sun's energy. The energy of the winds is most obvious during the vast tropical storms – hurricanes – that can destroy anything in their paths. But the weakest of winds, even drafts in houses, have the same cause – heat energy producing air movements.

This solar power station uses the Sun's energy to provide electricity. Large mirrors reflect the Sun's rays onto a central boiler.

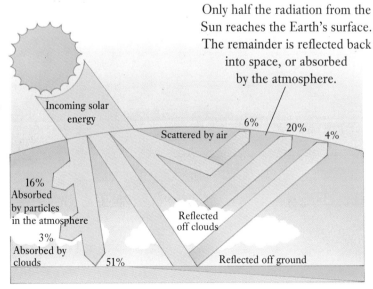

Only half the radiation from the Sun reaches the Earth's surface. The remainder is reflected back into space, or absorbed by the atmosphere.

Incoming solar energy

Scattered by air

6%   20%   4%

16% Absorbed by particles in the atmosphere

3% Absorbed by clouds

Reflected off clouds

51%

Reflected off ground

Plants use light energy from the Sun to produce food. Special pigments called chlorophylls absorb the Sun's energy and convert it to chemical energy, which is used to make sugars from carbon dioxide and water. This is called photosynthesis.

Wind power is increasingly being used to harness the energy of the atmosphere. These windmills in Altamont, California, each have a three-bladed propeller.

The steam engine illustrates how heat energy can be converted into movement. Coal is burned to heat up water and produce steam, which drives pistons to turn the wheels.

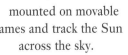

The mirrors are mounted on movable frames and track the Sun across the sky.

Sunny climes

Some places are cold, some are hot, and some have moderate temperatures. How hot a place is depends mainly upon how far it is from the equator. On average, it is hotter at low latitudes, near the equator, than in other parts of the world. At high latitudes, near the North and South Poles, the average temperature is a lot lower. This is because the Earth's surface is curved and so the Sun's rays are most concentrated at the equator. The opposite is true in polar regions: the Sun's rays are less concentrated because they are spread over a greater area of the globe. Also, the Sun's rays are weakened at the poles because they pass through a greater amount of atmosphere before reaching the ground. The climate, or the average weather conditions, at any place is affected by other things apart from the latitude. A warm ocean current flowing along a coast means a warmer climate for people living near the sea. A cold current has the opposite effect. Inland the climate may be quite different from that on the coast. The altitude, or height above sea level, also affects climate. The higher up a place is, the colder its climate will be.

Local climate depends on the height of an area. The lofty peak of Mount Kilimanjaro is near the equator but is covered with snow.

This satellite picture shows whirling masses of cloud over much of the world, but the hot desert belt in Africa has no cloud cover.

Heat is most concentrated when radiation from the Sun strikes the Earth at right angles. This means that the Sun's heat is concentrated at the equator, and is more spread out at the poles.

In deserts, there is no vegetation to reflect the Sun's heat. Most of the heat is absorbed and the desert is very hot. At night, the heat escapes from the land very quickly and it can be bitterly cold.

The World's Main Climate Zones

Cold forest
Tropical rainy
Temperate
Desert
Mountain
Polar

❏ Temperate climates are the most popular. Even though only 7 percent of the world enjoys a temperate climate, nearly half the world's people live in these areas.

❏ Quito in Ecuador, South America, is said to have the most pleasant climate in the world. It is called the 'Land of Eternal Spring.' The temperature rarely drops below 46°F (8°C) during the night, or exceeds 72°F (22°C) during the day.

❏ The bleakest places on Earth are the two poles: the South Pole has no sunshine for 182 days each year; the North Pole does slightly better, it has no sunlight on 176 days.

❏ The worst climate in the world may be at Yakutsk, in Russia. In winter, the temperature falls to −84°F (−64°C). In summer, it can reach 102°F (39°C).

❏ Small differences in height can make a big difference to the weather. Security guards on the top of the Empire State Building, New York, were able to make snowballs on November 3, 1958 while rain fell on 34th Street 1,250ft (381m) below.

The four seasons

Each year, the Earth makes its annual 600 million mile (965 million km) journey around the Sun. It takes 365 days 5 hours 48 minutes and 46 seconds to achieve one orbit of the Sun. Each day the Earth spins, or rotates, from west to east at a speed at the equator of nearly 1,050mph (1,700km/h). This west-to-east rotation causes night and day. The seasons arise because the Earth is tilted as it travels around the Sun. The Earth's axis of rotation – the 'axle' around which it spins – is tilted at an angle of 23.5 degrees in relation to the plane of its orbit. This means that, at certain times, some areas of the Earth are tilted away from the Sun and other areas are tilted toward the Sun. The northern hemisphere is tilted toward the Sun during the middle of the year, so June and July are warm summer months in the northern hemisphere. The southern hemisphere is tilted away from the Sun at this time, and so it is winter in southern lands at this time. Six months later the situation is reversed: it is summer in the southern hemisphere and winter in northern regions.

Deciduous trees grow in countries where the climate changes according to the season. The buds that appear in spring are able to withstand frost and snow.

By the summer months the young leaves inside the tough bud scales have opened out. Most broad-leaved trees in temperate regions are deciduous.

N

N

S

Northern summer/
southern winter

N

S

Southern summer/
northern winter

In between summer and winter, the Earth is not tilted toward the Sun. Days and nights are equal all over the world.

In the fall the supply of water and nutrients to the leaves stops. The leaves change color and die.

During summer in the southern hemisphere, the north pole is tipped away from the Sun.

❏ The Earth's orbit around the Sun is not perfectly circular; it is slightly oval-shaped. In the northern hemisphere, the Earth is about 3 million miles (5 million km) closer to the Sun during winter than in summer.

❏ If the Earth's axis was not tilted, there would be 12-hour days everywhere, and no seasons. At the poles, the Sun would be always on the horizon.

❏ On March 21 and September 22, when the Sun is vertical over the equator, day and night are of equal length. These times are called the equinoxes.

❏ Solstices are the two times each year, about 21 June and 21 December, when the Sun is furthest from the equator. At these times, there is maximum or minimum daylight in the two hemispheres.

❏ The planet Venus does not tilt as it goes around the Sun, so consequently it has no seasons. On Mars, however, the seasons are more exaggerated and last much longer than on Earth.

❏ The seventh planet from the Sun, Uranus, is tipped on its side so that at any moment one pole is pointed at the Sun. The polar regions are warmer than the equator. At the poles, a day lasts for 42 Earth years, followed by an equally long night.

Northern Finland is known as the Land of Midnight Sun. For weeks the Sun does not set.

During winter water in the soil may freeze. Deciduous trees survive by remaining dormant.

Blue skies and rainbows

Sunlight or white light is a mixture of colors: red, orange, yellow, green, blue, indigo, violet – all the colors of the rainbow. If a thin beam of white light or sunlight is passed through a triangle-shaped piece of glass, called a prism, the colors are separated and easily seen. Rainbows also reveal the colorful nature of sunlight. They occur when sunlight passes through raindrops in such a way that the light is split into its colors. To form a rainbow, light must enter a raindrop from the front, be reflected off the back of raindrop, and then out into the air again. The blue of the daytime sky also arises from the colors of sunlight. If you look at the sky near the Sun (never look directly at the Sun!) the sky seems slightly yellow. This is because the white sunlight has had some blue light removed from it. The blue light is scattered, or bounced off, air particles and so most does not reach your eyes. The blue light in sunlight is scattered more strongly than other colors, and so blue light is lost as the sunlight travels to your eyes. The remaining unscattered light appears slightly yellow. If you look at other parts of the sky, there is no direct sunlight and you only see the scattered blue light. So, the sky appears blue in these directions.

Sometimes a less intense secondary rainbow, in which the colors are reversed, forms outside the main one.

The best time to see a rainbow is in the afternoon on a rainy day. Look at the raindrops with the Sun behind you.

White light passing through a glass prism. The stripe of colors produced is called a spectrum.

The spectrum given out when a substance is heated can be used to identify the components of that substance. This scientist is working with a spectrometer, which displays the spectrum of light given out by a heated material.

The beautiful colors of a sunset are the result of the scattering of blue light.

❏ A green flash is sometimes seen just as the Sun sets or rises. This is caused because green light is bent most strongly by the atmosphere. So the green is seen before other colors at sunrise, and after the other colors have vanished at sunset.

❏ The Moon may appear to be blue when smoke particles high in the atmosphere scatter red light more than blue. These conditions do not happen very often, hence the expression 'once in a blue moon.'

❏ A rainbow seen in North Wales by Kathleen Mills of Manchester, England, on August 14, 1979 lasted over three hours, the longest lasting rainbow ever recorded.

Pictures in the sky

Have you noticed that a drinking straw, resting in a glass of water, seems to be bent? This happens because light travelling from the straw is bent, or refracted, as it passes from the water to the air around the glass. Water and air have different densities, and so light travels at different speeds in them. This causes a light ray to bend when it travels from air into water. Light rays can be bent in the same way as they pass through the atmosphere. Where a light ray passes from a dense layer of the atmosphere to a less dense layer, the ray is bent. Mirages are caused in this way. If air near the ground is hotter than the air higher up, light rays are bent so that distant objects appear to be lower than they really are. In a desert, blue light from the sky may appear to come from ground level, and so we might think it was water. If air near the ground is colder than air above, light rays are bent in the opposite ways, but mirages can still be seen. For example, ghostly mountains often appear in the sky over the Gulf of California, just before sunset. As the sea breeze over the Gulf dies down, an hour or so before sunset, cold air settles over the Gulf. This causes a mirage of the 10,130ft (3,088m) peak of Cerro de la Encantada on the Baja California peninsula to be visible on the other side of the Gulf, 116 miles (186km) away. The mirage is quite clear, making it seem that the mountains have grown to four times their normal size.

The narrow strip of water in which the giraffes appear to be standing is a mirage.

The Northern Lights flicker in the sky above Finland. The lights are caused by huge eruptions on the Sun, which discharge particles into the upper atmosphere.

Light can play tricks on our eyes! Here a toothbrush appears to vanish when held in water. This happens because the brush handle is made of a material which refracts light in exactly the same way as water does.

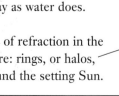

The effects of refraction in the atmosphere: rings, or halos, appear around the setting Sun.

The neon lights of Hong Kong are like the lights of an aurora. Both are caused by glowing gas.

❑ The largest mirage ever seen was sighted in the Arctic in 1913 by Donald MacMillan. Hills, valleys, and mountain peaks were seen stretching across most of the horizon. The same mirage was probably seen by polar explorer Robert Peary six years earlier when he mistakenly reported a large island at the same position.

❑ A beautiful mirage called the Fata Morgana appears in the Straits of Messina, between Sicily and Italy. It is an image of a town in the sky, but it seems more like a fairy landscape than a real town. People in white seem to walk through the streets. Probably it is a mirage of a fishing village situated along the coast.

❑ The Sun can sometimes seem to be square to Eskimos and Arctic explorers. The effect is probably seen when adjacent layers of air bend light rays both horizontally and vertically.

❑ A 'cloud map' is a reflection of light from the land seen on the underside of a cloud layer. The color of the reflected light reveals if the land surface is covered with water, snow, or ice. Cloud maps can be used as aids to navigation, leading travellers along open passages of water in an ice sheet, for example.

Air on the move

Winds flow because of pressure differences in the atmosphere. When atmospheric pressure is high, air is squashed together. The squashed, high-pressure air tends to flow toward places where the pressure is lower. It is easy to demonstrate that air flows out of high-pressure regions: blow up a balloon, and then release it. The balloon flies around the room because high-pressure air inside the balloon is being expelled, creating a small jet or wind. The pressure of the atmosphere at ground level is not the same all over the world because some places are hotter than others. For example, the inland regions of continents are hot in summer. This causes the air to rise – warm air rises because it expands. As the air rises, it does not press so heavily on the ground. This creates an area of low pressure into which winds blow. In winter, air above the inland regions of continents is cold and sinks down, pressing more heavily on the ground. This creates an area of high pressure away from which winds blow. However, the pressure at any place is not constant. It changes as air flows from one region to another, or as one region warms and another cools. Thus, there is a changing pattern of high and low pressure over the Earth. However, within this pattern there are unchanging features: a band of constant low pressure at the equator, and a region of permanent high pressure at the poles. This pattern creates the world's winds.

A pneumatic drill is operated by compressed air. Pulses of compressed air force the drill downward, proving that high pressure can produce movement.

Hot air expands. Spread soapy lather across the top of a bottle. Warm the bottle with your hands. The air inside expands and makes a bubble.

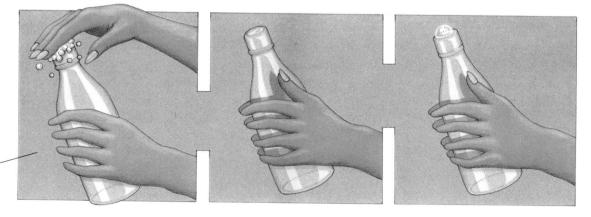

30

The Space Shuttle is propelled upward into space by the pressure of gases expelled by the engines underneath the craft.

The pressure in a bottle of champagne drives a spray of frothy liquid and gas into the air. Weather systems also 'pop their corks,' blowing giant sprays of air and water vapor across the world.

❏ The highest air pressure ever recorded was 1,083.8 millibars at Agata, Siberia, eastern Russia.

❏ The lowest air pressure recorded at sea level was at Guam, in the Pacific Ocean, on October 12, 1979. A pressure of only 870 millibars was recorded in the center of typhoon *Tip*.

❏ There is a belt of semi-permanent low pressure at the equator. There is semi-permanent high pressure at latitudes 30°N and 30°S. Small areas around the poles always have high air pressure.

❏ Air pressure rises from 4 a.m. to 10 a.m., falls from 10 a.m. to 4 p.m., rises between 4 p.m. and 10 p.m., and then drops from 10 p.m. to 4 a.m. These changes mirror temperature changes during the day and night, although they may be disguised by pressure changes caused by passing weather systems.

❏ An air-pressure rise or fall of 10 millibars in 3 hours is a sure sign of a coming gale. In September 1900, when a hurricane hit Galveston, Texas, the pressure fell by about 22 millibars in 4 hours.

❏ The weight of air pressing down on us at sea level is equal to the weight of a small car. We do not notice it because within our bodies there is an equal force pressing outward.

Breezes and winds

Hot air in a balloon is less dense than the air around it and so the balloon rises.

Bubbles of hot air are continually rising over hot areas, such as hillside slopes that catch the sunlight, or cities that generate heat. High above the ground, the air cools. It sinks toward the ground. A continuous circulation can be set up with hot air rising, cooling, and falling to be heated once again. These circulations are called convection currents. Such currents occur not just in the atmosphere – where, of course, they are called winds or breezes – but wherever liquids and gases are heated. They are found in cofee cups, saucepans, oceans, and inside the Sun. Convection currents can be large scale, moving air over great distances, or they can be smaller, local breezes. At the equator, hot air rises and, high above the ground, flows toward the poles. Eventually, the air cools and sinks to the ground. The cool air then moves back toward the equator. Hence, there are steady winds, called the trade winds, blowing toward the equator. Land and sea breezes are convection currents on a smaller scale. On a hot sunny day, air above the land heats up more quickly than air above the sea. This causes air to rise over the land and cooler air from the sea to flow inland. At night, the situation is reversed, and the breeze blows from the land to the sea.

Rising currents of warm air, or thermals, often reach 10,000ft (3,000m). Birds with large wingspans use thermals to gain height. This is a Bald eagle; its wingspan can be as great as 90in (2.3m) across.

During the day air above the land warms up and rises. Cool air from the sea flows in, so causing onshore breezes.

At night the situation is reversed. The land cools faster than the sea, so the flow of air is off the land out to sea.

An open parawing fills with rising air. The parachutist learns to find rising currents of air, and uses these to stay aloft.

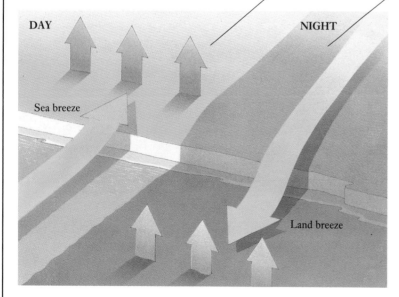

DAY   NIGHT

Sea breeze

Land breeze

The hot air in a balloon is generated by a gas burner. When the balloon cools it will descend, completing a small convection current.

Convection currents carry heat away from the hot spot that created them. In this image of a boiled kettle the white areas show where the water is hottest.

A basket, or car, below the balloon carries the pilot, passengers, and equipment. Unmanned balloons can carry weather-recording instruments.

❑ The world's windiest place is reputed to be Commonwealth Bay, George V Coast, Antarctica, where wind speeds of 200mph (320km/h) have been recorded.

❑ The highest wind speed recorded at ground level is 230mph (371km/h) at Mt. Washington, New Hampshire, on April 12, 1934. The winds were three times as fast as those in a hurricane.

❑ The mistral wind of southern France once blew a string of locomotive cars from Arles to Port-St.-Louis 25 miles (40km) away before the cars could be stopped.

❑ In California, winds from the Pacific blow across the Rockies from the west. Rain falls on the west slope of the mountains; a hot wind called the Chinook blows down the east slopes. The Chinook wind is called the 'snow eater.' It is so warm that it can melt a foot of snow in a few minutes.

❑ A wind farm at Altamont Pass, California, consists of 300 wind turbines. To produce as much electricity as a nuclear power station, a wind farm would need to occupy an area of around 140 square miles (370 km^2).

❑ The world's largest wind generator is on the island of Oahu, Hawaii. The windmill has two blades 400ft (122m) long on the top of a tower, twenty stories high.

Water – the essential liquid

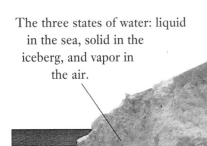

A vapor trail. Water vapor in the jet's exhaust has come into contact with the cold air and condensed.

Water is the most common substance on Earth. More than three-quarters of the surface of the globe is covered with water, and if there were no water there would be no weather. Water is the only substance on Earth that occurs naturally as a solid, liquid, and gas (or vapor). All air contains varying amounts of water vapor, although we cannot see the vapor – it is invisible. Steam and fog are not water vapor; these are minute drops of liquid water suspended in the air.

Water vapor can change, or condense, to liquid water. Liquid water can boil or evaporate to form vapor, and can freeze to ice. Ice can melt to produce liquid water. Heat energy is absorbed or given out when these changes take place. Heat energy is absorbed by melting ice, for example. Energy is also absorbed when water evaporates or boils to form vapor. The reverse changes release energy. When water vapor condenses or liquid water freezes, heat energy is released. This means that water vapor is an efficient 'heat carrier.' The vapor absorbs heat when it is formed from water, and releases the heat when it condenses back to water. Because of this effect, winds carrying water vapor transport heat more efficiently than dry winds.

The three states of water: liquid in the sea, solid in the iceberg, and vapor in the air.

If ice sank instead of floating, the polar seas would be permanently frozen, and the world's weather would be very different.

When warm air inside a room strikes a cold window pane the water vapor in the air condenses.

Water vapor in the atmosphere accounts for about 3 percent of the mass of the air.

When salt water is heated, the water evaporates to form vapor; the salt remains behind. This desalination plant on Lake Mead, Nevada, extracts salt from water by evaporation.

This false-color satellite image of the Earth shows the water vapor in the atmosphere. Air can only hold a certain amount of water vapor. If there is too much, it condenses to form a cloud.

❏ The oceans contain 97 percent of the water on Earth; about three-quarters of the rest is locked into ice sheets and glaciers, the remainder is stored in the soil, underground reservoirs, and the atmosphere. The atmosphere contains only one part in ten thousand of all global water.

❏ About two-thirds of the world's fresh water flows out of the Amazon River in South America. The amount discharged is so immense that fresh water can be found on the sea surface 40 miles (64km) from the river's mouth.

❏ The total volume of water on Earth is estimated to be 310 million cubic miles (about 1,384 million km^3), enough for each person on Earth to have 270 million baths.

❏ Ice always starts to melt at 32°F (0°C). As the ice melts, heat is absorbed, but the heat is used entirely for melting the ice and not for raising the temperature of the mixture of ice and water. The temperature remains constant at 32°F (0°C) until all the ice has melted.

❏ Melting ice absorbs almost as much energy in changing to liquid water as is needed to heat the water from freezing to boiling.

❏ Boiling water absorbs over six times more energy in changing to steam than is needed to heat the water from freezing to boiling.

Water's endless cycle

Each drop of rain that falls has fallen millions of times before. It is taking part in an endless cycle, called the water cycle. At stage one, the water is in the sea. Overhead the Sun shines down, heating the water. Water vapor is drawn into the air by evaporation. Perhaps wind then blows the vapor inland and up a mountain slope. As the vapor rises, it cools, and condenses back into water. Rain falls on the mountainside, and runs back into the sea by rivers and streams. The cycle is complete. In tropical coastal areas, water can run through the water cycle in one hour; in the Arctic it can take tens of thousands of years to complete the same process. The water cycle combines convection currents – flows of heated air – with the evaporation and condensation of water. This combination is a very efficient way of transferring heat from one place to another. Not only is heat carried along by the hot air, but the water vapor also carries heat – its latent heat. The water vapor gains latent heat when it evaporates from the sea; in the process, the sea is cooled. When the vapor condenses, the latent heat is released, heating the nearby air. Exactly the same process is used in a refrigerator to pump heat from the stored food and into the air surrounding the machine.

Water is being constantly recycled. It evaporates from the sea, lakes, soil, and plants and returns to the sea in rivers, and seepage through the ground.

Direct evaporation

Evaporation from sea

The Sun, the driving force of the water cycle, draws water from the sea, forming clouds.

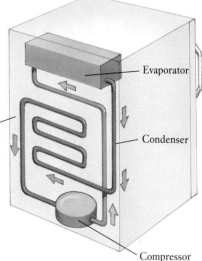

A fluid called the refrigerant circulates through the pipes of a refrigerator. The refrigerant changes from a liquid to a gas inside the evaporator, absorbing heat as it does so. The gas is compressed and changed back to a liquid in the exterior pipes.

Evaporator

Condenser

Compressor

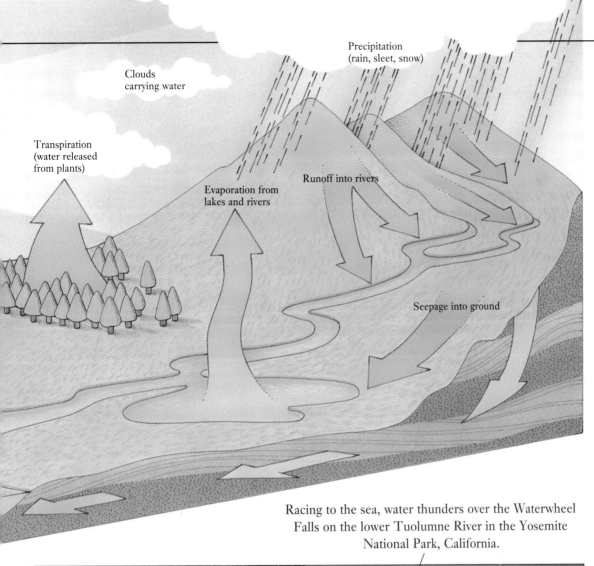

Clouds
carrying water

Transpiration
(water released
from plants)

Precipitation
(rain, sleet, snow)

Evaporation from
lakes and rivers

Runoff into rivers

Seepage into ground

Racing to the sea, water thunders over the Waterwheel
Falls on the lower Tuolumne River in the Yosemite
National Park, California.

❏ One-third of the solar energy reaching the Earth is used in evaporating water: about 95,000 cubic miles (380,000km³) each year. This is the equivalent of 30 lakes the size of Lake Superior.

❏ Over one year, up to 79in (200cm) of water evaporates from the western Pacific and central Indian Oceans. If no rain fell over these seas, and no water entered the seas from rivers, the sea level would drop by an equivalent 79in (200cm) each year.

❏ The total water content of the oceans on Earth would take one million years to be cycled through the atmosphere as part of the water cycle.

❏ On a hot afternoon, the atmosphere draws up 5,500 million gallons (21,000 million liters) of water an hour from the Gulf of Mexico.

❏ A drop of water may travel thousands of miles between the time it evaporates into the atmosphere and the time it falls to Earth again as rain, sleet, or snow.

❏ Every day 8.25 million tons (8 million tonnes) of water evaporates from the Dead Sea, on the border between Israel and Jordan.

❏ Hot air can contain more water than cold air. In the tropics, air can hold as much water vapor as the air in a sauna bath.

Weather fronts

There are parts of the world, such as the oceans and the inland parts of large continents, where conditions are similar over great areas. Over these areas, huge masses of air develop in which the temperature and moisture content is uniform. The air may be warm or cold, dry or moist, depending upon the area of land or sea it forms over. These air masses drift over the Earth's surface, bringing a change of weather as they move to a new location. The boundaries between air masses are called fronts. Near a front, the weather is unsettled and changeable, with clouds, rain, and storms. There are three types of front: warm, cold, and occluded. In a warm front, warm air moves into an area occupied by cold air. Because the warm air is less dense, it slides over and above the cold air, producing clouds as it rises. Often, steady prolonged rain falls ahead of the warm air. In a cold front, cold air moves towards warmer air. The denser cold air slides under the warm air. Once again, clouds are produced as the warm air is forced upward. A short spell of heavy rain often occurs, followed by brighter, showery weather. An occluded front occurs when a cold front overtakes a warm front. The cold front lifts the warm front, and results in a warm front that does not touch the ground. Steady rain is produced, usually followed by brighter weather. Fronts, then, bring stormy, changeable weather. Fixed air masses mean stable climatic conditions.

Hot, muggy weather in New York, as a mass of tropical air from the Caribbean moves in.

An approaching cold front, marked by a line of cloud. As the front passes overhead, there is a rise in pressure and the temperature drops.

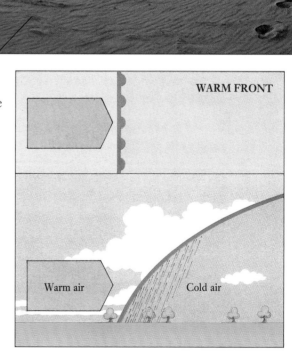

WARM FRONT

Warm air

Cold air

COLD FRONT

Cold air

Warm air

In a warm front (left), a wide band of clouds and rain arrives before the mass of warm air. A narrow band of cloud and rain accompanies a cold front (above). A wide band of rain and cloud accompanies an occluded front (right) where a cold front is overtaking a warm front.

OCCLUDED FRONT

Warm air

Cold air

Cool air

❑ Strange though it may seem, the air over the equator can be colder than that over the poles. In 1957 a temperature of −146°F (−99°C) was measured 7 miles (11km) above the Maldive Islands in the tropical Indian Ocean. At these heights, a temperature of −40°F (−40°C) is considered warm.

❑ Air masses can cover vast areas, up to 3 million square miles (7 million km²), about the size of Brazil.

❑ A cold front travels at a speed of about 30mph (50km/h) – faster than the fastest person can run – and may overtake any warm front ahead of it. The resulting mix of air is called an occluded front.

❑ A polar air mass moving south from Canada may pick up from the Mississippi basin more than nine times as much water as flows out from the mouth of the river.

❑ Distinct bands of rainy weather and clouds can form up to 240 miles (386km) ahead of warm fronts. These bands are parallel to the front, and are often about 125 miles (200km) long and 30 miles (48km) wide.

Weather charts

Weather charts reveal the pattern of the weather at a particular time. The chart shows the air pressure, winds, temperature, cloud cover, rainfall and humidity, usually at ground level. Weather map symbols are internationally agreed and can be seen on weather maps all around the world. Continuous lines called isobars are drawn on the chart to join places of equal sea level air pressure. Areas of high pressure, called anticyclones, are marked with an H, for 'high.' Areas of low pressure are called cyclones or depressions. They are marked with an L, for 'low.' Wind speed and direction are indicated by arrow-like symbols on weather charts. Winds blow approximately along isobars. Winds blowing around a low-pressure area actually blow slightly across the isobars, toward the low pressure. Around a high-pressure area, the winds blow slightly across the isobars, away from the high pressure. In the northern hemisphere, the winds blow clockwise around a high, and anticlockwise around a low. In the southern hemisphere, the winds blow in opposite directions. A warm front is indicated by a line with small semicircles attached. A cold front is indicated by a line with triangles attached, and an occluded front by a line with alternate triangles and semicircles. Fronts are usually found near areas of high or low pressure. Other special symbols indicate cloud cover, rain, snow, fog, thunderstorms and other details of the weather.

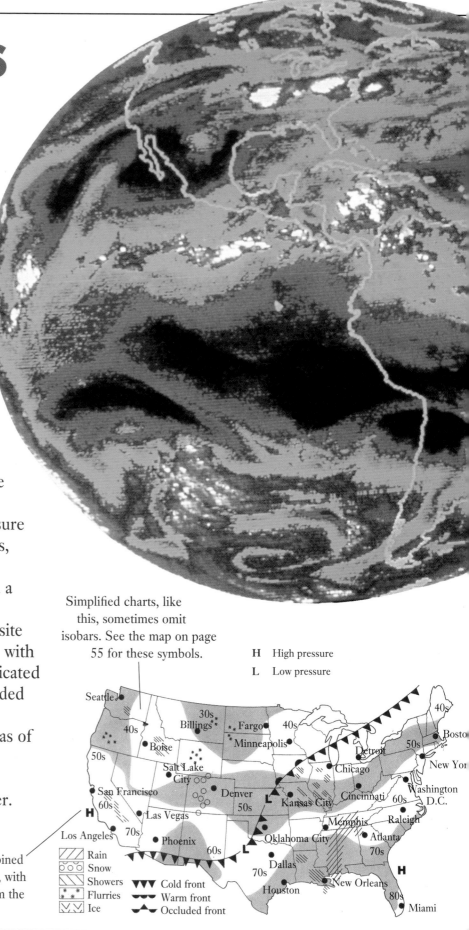

Simplified charts, like this, sometimes omit isobars. See the map on page 55 for these symbols.

H   High pressure
L   Low pressure

Weather map for November 14, 1991. A combined cold and occluded front lies across the country, with scattered areas of rain. Temperatures vary from the 80s in Florida to the 30s in Montana.

Rain
Snow
Showers
Flurries
Ice

▼▼▼ Cold front
▼▼ Warm front
▲▲ Occluded front

Watching the weather by satellite means more accurate weather maps and predictions. This image shows the temperature and moisture over the Americas.

Weather records have been kept for centuries. These are the daily records for Chelmsford, England, for June 1770.

A severe depression or cyclone forming over northern Europe. Really, depressions should be called 'extratropical cyclones' to distinguish them from the storms, also called cyclones, that occur in the Indian Ocean.

Meteorologist studying a weather satellite image at the U.S. National Weather and Hurricane Service.

❏ The invention and development of the telegraph in the 1840s made possible the swift collection of information from widespread weather stations, and thus enabled the first weather maps to be drawn.

❏ The first synoptic weather chart was produced in 1842 by Elias Loomis at Yale University, New Haven, Connecticut. 'Synoptic' means 'seen together.' Synoptic charts show the weather at a particular moment.

❏ In 1758, Swiss-German scientist Johann Heinrich Lambert (1728-1777) published a weather book, using symbols borrowed from medieval astronomers. Signs such as these came into widespread use in the 18th century and were the forerunners of modern weather symbols.

❏ The world's first television weather chart was broadcast in Britain on November 11, 1936.

Tornadoes – spirals of destruction

A crop circle in southern England. One theory supposes that these are caused by small whirlpools of air.

Whirling motions, called vortices, are the most efficient method found in Nature of shifting liquids and gases in a hurry. Water flows down a whirlpool, or a bath plughole, swiftly because it speeds up as it spirals inward. This is an example of the 'spinning skater effect:' as a spinning skater draws in her arms, she turns more rapidly. In the atmosphere, this effect produces spinning storms – tornadoes – with winds reaching speeds as high as 280mph (450km/h). Tornadoes, or 'twisters,' start when an updraft of air in a thundercloud is set spinning by winds in the upper part of the cloud. Air is sucked into the spinning column at the bottom. The air speeds up as it spirals toward the center of the column, increasing the strength of the updraft. The column grows, reaching down from the cloud bottom, until it touches the ground. The violent updraft inside the column acts like a giant vacuum cleaner, sucking in dust, ripping the roofs off buildings, lifting cars, people – and entire buildings – into the sky. The column speeds across the land, leaving behind a narrow trail of destruction. Water spouts are similar spinning storms that occur over the seas, sucking up water. Over deserts, spinning air columns produce dust devils.

Aircraft overturned during a tornado in Louisiana.

❏ In 1981, a tornado lifted a baby from its pram in the Italian city of Ancona. The baby was carried 50ft (15m) into the air and set down safely 300ft (90m) away – without waking!

❏ In 1950, a tornado plucked some chickens from their coop in Bedfordshire, England. The chickens were plucked in more than one sense – their feathers exploded because the normal air pressure inside the quills was much higher than the low pressure air of the tornado.

❏ During a tornado in Ponca City, Oklahoma, a man and his wife were carried aloft in their house by a tornado. The walls and roof were blown away, but the floor remained intact and eventually glided downward, setting the couple safely back on the ground.

❏ The most destructive tornado on record occurred in Annapolis, Missouri. In three hours, it tore through the town on March 18, 1925 leaving a 980-foot (300m)-wide trail of demolished buildings, uprooted trees, and overturned cars. It left 823 people dead and almost 3,000 injured.

Water spout in the Mediterranean. They are usually between 165 and 330 feet (50-100m) high.

In deserts, strong whirlwinds are called dust devils. They are usually about 100ft (30m) high.

Tornado damage in Kentucky. Buildings explode as a twister passes over them.

Tornado in Texas. A wind speed of 280mph (450km/h) was measured in a tornado at Wichita Falls, Texas in 1958.

Hurricanes, cyclones, and typhoons

The most violent and powerful storms are called hurricanes, typhoons, or tropical cyclones. These storms begin over the warm tropical seas and cause great destruction if they move on to the land. When the storms develop in the Atlantic Ocean or Caribbean they are called hurricanes. In the Pacific Ocean they are called typhoons, and in the Indian Ocean they are known as tropical cyclones. In these storms, very strong winds circle around a region of low air pressure. Surprisingly, in the center of these immense storms, there is a small quiet area called the 'eye.' In the eye, the sky is clear of cloud and only a light breeze is blowing. However, just outside the quiet eye, the full power of the hurricane is felt. Wind speeds may reach 220mph (360km/h), powerful enough to drive a plank of wood through the trunk of a tree. Torrential rain pours down, the seas rage with giant waves whipped up by the winds. Hurricanes, typhoons, and tropical cyclones may measure as much as 480 miles (800km) across. It can take 18 hours for such large storms to pass over a coastal town on their journey inland.

30°N

Equator

30°S

Hurricane zones

Hurricanes develop over warm waters close to, but not on, the equator. The main development areas are in the western Atlantic, and right across the tropical Pacific and Indian oceans. They normally arise during the months of July to October.

The eye of the storm is visible near the center, with swirling bands of high-level cloud spiralling outward.

Hurricane *Carol* lashing the east coast of America. Although its power is awesome, the storm is now approaching its end.

A tropical cyclone over Timor in Indonesia, photographed from a Space Shuttle. Winds reached speeds of 70mph (110km/h).

A computer-colored satellite photograph of hurricane *Allen* over the Gulf of Mexico on August 8, 1980. Its spiral form is evident.

Shuttle photograph of a storm near the Gulf of Mexico. The southern coastline of Texas on the border with Mexico can be seen bottom left.

The areas of high-level cloud, which is very cold, show up as dark red. Low-level clouds are pink.

Inside a hurricane

A hurricane is a huge natural engine. Like all engines, it produces movement from a fuel. However, a hurricane is a very peculiar engine, because it supplies itself with fuel. The fuel is water vapor drawn from the sea. Hurricanes start over warm tropical seas when winds from opposite directions meet, causing an upward spiral of air. Water vapor, drawn from the warm sea, is carried aloft. As the water vapor rises, it condenses to form clouds. Heat energy is released as the vapor condenses, warming the air. As the air is warmed, it rises even faster. The updraft begins to act like a chimney, drawing air in at the bottom and blowing it out the top. Another mechanism helps to increase wind speeds in the developing hurricane. As air is drawn in toward the updraft, it moves in a spiral path. The air speeds up as it spirals inward just as the winds in a tornado speed up as they spiral inward. This increases the speed of the air going 'up the chimney.' So, even more water vapor is drawn upward, and even more heat energy is released. A chain reaction is established, releasing increasing amounts of energy, and producing increasingly violent winds. The hurricane become self-sustaining. It will die out only if it moves over land, where there is no supply of its vital fuel, water vapor.

The high-level winds spiral outward from the center of the storm. Inside the eye, cold air descends.

A rising column of warm moist air surrounds the eye of the hurricane.

Jupiter's thick atmosphere flows around the Red Spot, a spiral storm which has been raging for over 300 years.

The Red Spot on Jupiter is actually larger than the Earth.

46

Satellite view of hurricane *Allen* over the Gulf of Mexico on August 8, 1980. The eye can be clearly seen.

A satellite photograph of a severe storm in the Bering Sea on April 2, 1978. The high-level clouds spiral outward from the eye.

The eye of the hurricane, looking upward. The clear air in the eye, and the wall of cloud surrounding it, can be seen.

The water vapor in the rising air condenses to produce clouds and heavy rain at the base of the storm.

Tropical winds

A ship lies becalmed in the doldrums – a belt of still air lying between the bands of the trade winds.

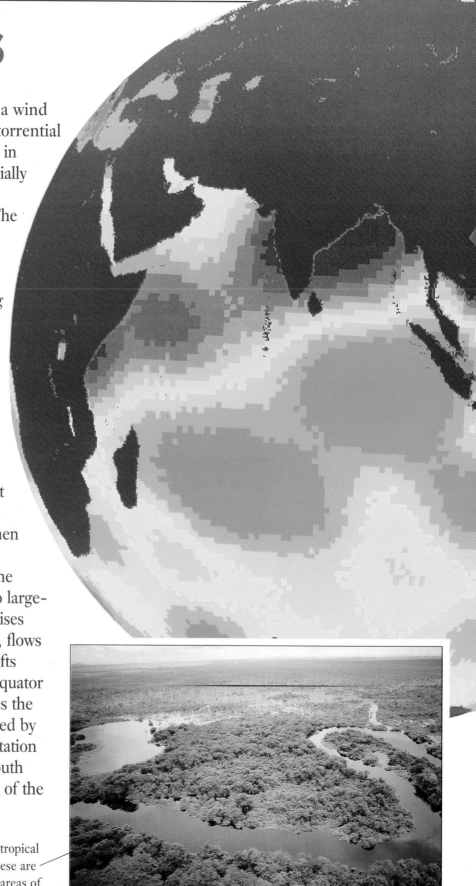

A monsoon is a wind that brings torrential rain and flooding in the tropics, especially to India and southeast Asia. The monsoon sweeps in across India during the summer, bringing moisture-laden air from the Indian Ocean. During winter, the wind reverses and cold dry air flows southwest from Asia, across India, and out over the ocean. The monsoon is a very powerful sea and land breeze. The continents of India and Asia heat up in summer and as a result huge convection currents rise above the land. Moist air flows in from the ocean, creating the rain-bearing summer monsoon. During winter, when the land is colder than the sea, the process is reversed. The trade winds that blow toward the equator over the oceans of the tropics are also large-scale convection currents. Warm tropical air rises near the equator and, high in the atmosphere, flows toward the poles. Eventually, the air cools, drifts downward, and some flows back toward the equator at ground level. This ground-level flow creates the trade winds. However, the flow of air is affected by the west-to-east rotation of the Earth. The rotation deflects the trade winds from a strict north-south course, and, as a result, the trade winds north of the equator blow from the northeast, while the trade winds in the southern hemisphere blow from a southeast direction.

Rainy season in the tropical Brazilian forest. These are amongst the wettest areas of the world.

Satellite map of winds over the Pacific Ocean. The arrows represent wind direction and the colors indicate wind speed. Blue indicates the slowest winds, and yellow the fastest. Notice the two intense circular storms east of New Zealand.

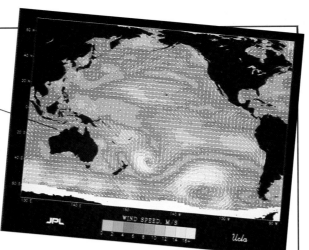

❏ The monsoons bring the heaviest rain in the world. The greatest amount of rain to fall in one month is 366in (9,300mm), which fell during July 1861 at Cherrapunji, India. Cherrapunji also holds the record for the most rain in a year, 1,041in (26,461mm) from August 1, 1860 to July 31, 1861.

Columbus' voyages were made possible by the trade winds.

Computer-colored satellite image showing variations in air pressure around the Indian Ocean during winter. The red areas show where the air pressure is low. Monsoon winds blow toward these areas.

The trade winds are caused by giant circular currents of air near the equator. This circulation is called the Hadley cell, after George Hadley, an 18th century London lawyer who first studied it. The ground-level winds flowing toward the equator, called the trade winds, are deflected by the rotation of the Earth.

High pressure

Polar cell

Low pressure

North pole

High pressure

Hadley cell

Mid-latitude westerlies

Northeast trade winds

Low pressure

Equator

Southeast trade winds

Mid-latitude westerlies

South pole

❏ Columbus might never have sighted America in 1492 without the help of the trade winds that blew him across the Atlantic. In 1492 the trade winds had veered unusually far to the north, and Columbus was able to travel about 100 miles (160km) a day with their help.

❏ The word 'monsoon' is derived from the Arabic word 'mausim' meaning season. It was first used by Arab sailors to describe the seasonal winds that blow across the Arabian Sea.

The restless ocean

The oceans are an important part of the global weather machine. After all, seven-tenths of the world's surface is covered by water. Because water is such an efficient heat store, the oceans store far more energy than the atmosphere. This heat is carried away from the warm tropical regions by ocean currents, helping to balance the global distribution of heat. The surface ocean currents are generated by the winds. For this reason, they move in the same general direction as the winds. There are two clockwise circulations in the northern hemisphere – in the North Atlantic and the North Pacific. In the southern oceans, there are three anticlockwise circular currents – in the southern Pacific Ocean, the southern Atlantic Ocean, and the southern Indian Ocean. Although ocean currents are slow-moving compared to winds, they can carry huge amounts of water and energy. The Gulf Stream carries 1,050 million cubic feet (30 million m^3) of water northward along the Florida coast every second, and the water is 14°F (8°C) warmer than the water that returns south along the European and African coasts.

Warm currents
Cold currents

Surface ocean currents circulate in the same direction as the winds. There are two large clockwise circulations in the northern hemisphere, in the north Atlantic and the north Pacific. In the southern hemisphere, there are three anticlockwise circulations, in the Pacific, Indian, and Atlantic Oceans.

Rough seas. The wind whipping up the seas is part of a natural system which balances the global distribution of energy.

As you go deeper in the ocean, the colder the water gets. In deep water the temperature may be only 36°F (2°C). At the surface, the temperature may reach 86°F (30°C) in the tropics.

Satellite image showing the temperature of the sea surface along the eastern U.S. seaboard. The Gulf Stream (pink) is clearly visible.

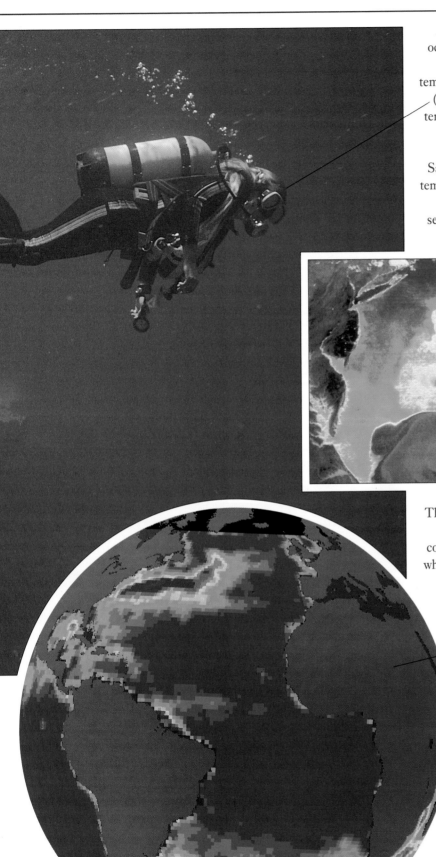

The warm Gulf Stream flows northward. The sea fogs common in this region occur when it meets cold air flowing south from the Arctic.

Computer-colored satellite image showing the main ocean currents in the Atlantic Ocean. Swiftly-moving waters are shown in red.

The Agulhas Current flows south between Madagascar and the east African coast, rounding the tip of Africa. Across the Atlantic, the West Wind Drift forms a circular eddy near South America.

Winds on a spinning world

The English meteorologist George Hadley (1685-1768).

One of the keys to understanding the weather machine is to remember that the Earth is spinning, or rotating, west to east. The spin of the Earth, of course, causes day and night. In 1735, an English lawyer, George Hadley, realized that the spin also causes winds to veer off their expected course. Hadley recognized that an object on the equator was moving eastward at a high speed. Furthermore, another object nearer the pole had a lesser distance to travel as the Earth rotated, and so must move more slowly. Thus, Hadley reasoned that air that blew south toward the equator starts off with too little eastward speed to keep pace with the spinning Earth near the equator. The air will lag behind, and seem to veer in toward the equator from the northeast. This is the reason that the trade winds blow from the northeast in the northern hemisphere. In the southern hemisphere, the trade winds blow from the southeast for the same reason. In the same way, a wind blowing north from the equator has too much eastward speed to flow directly north. It veers eastward because of its extra eastward speed. The further north the wind goes, the more easterly becomes its direction. By the time the wind has gone about one-third of the way to the pole, it is blowing directly toward the east. This is why there are almost always winds blowing toward the east across Europe and North America. Since winds are named by the direction from which they blow, these winds are called westerlies. Similar westerlies blow in the southern hemisphere, too.

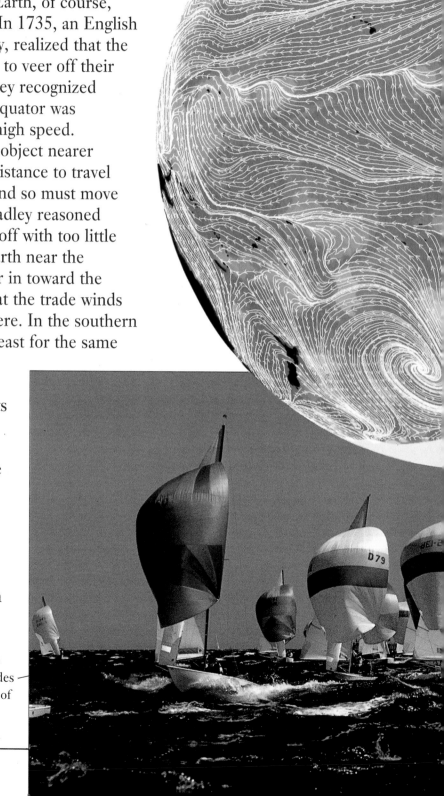

Sailors must understand the winds. Even winds like the trades vary with the season, the time of day, and local conditions.

A satellite image of the world's winds. The trade winds can be seen blowing toward the equator. The region between the trade winds and the poles is turbulent and contains many spiral air flows.

Rockets are usually launched from near the equator to take advantage of the Earth's spin.

Mosaic image of global weather produced by the Tiros 9 satellite on February 13, 1965. This was the first complete view of the Earth's weather systems.

The world's weather systems are rather like the cooling system of an automobile. Water carries excess heat from the engine to the radiator. In this way, the engine is kept from overheating. In the same way, winds carry excess heat away from the equator toward the poles, and so regulate the temperature.

❑ The spin of the Earth means that at the equator everything is moving through space at a speed of 1,000mph (1,600km/h), even when standing still on the ground. Space launch sites are situated near the equator so that they can take advantage of this fact. The spin of the Earth gives rockets extra momentum at lift-off.

❑ An aircraft flying from Seattle, on the northwest coast of America, to Florida, in the southeast, would actually land in Mexico if the pilot did not make allowance for the rotation of the Earth when navigating.

❑ The sea level at the Pacific end of the Panama canal is lower than sea level at the Caribbean end. This is due to the rotation of the Earth, which piles up water on the eastern side of the American land mass as the Earth turns from west to east.

❑ Long-range artillery must allow for the deflection of their shells by the Earth's rotation when calculating trajectories. Like the winds, the shells are deflected toward the right in the northern hemisphere, and to the left in the southern hemisphere.

❑ Rivers in the northern hemisphere scour their right-hand banks more severely than their left-hand banks. This effect is due to the rotation of the Earth.

53

The changeable westerlies

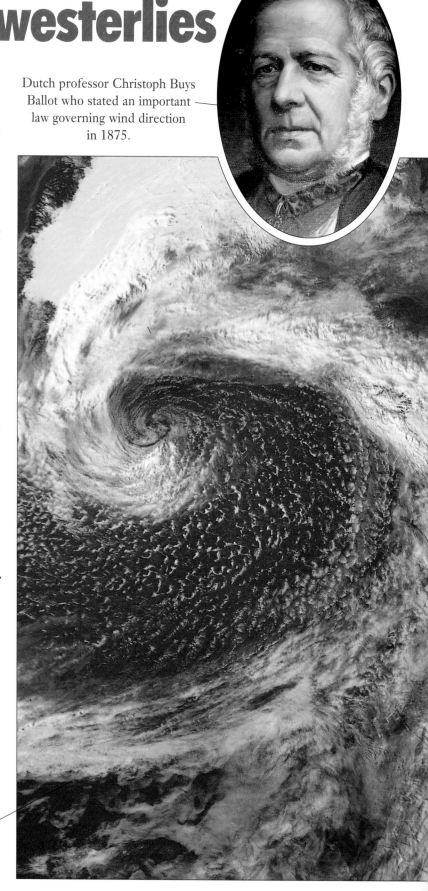

Dutch professor Christoph Buys Ballot who stated an important law governing wind direction in 1875.

The weather is always changing. This is especially true in middle latitudes – about halfway between the equator and the poles – where the westerly winds blow. In these regions, cold air from the poles meets and mixes with warm tropical air. The result is turbulent air flow, with areas of low and high pressure forming and being carried along by the westerlies. Low pressure areas form at the polar front, where cold dry polar air meets warm moist tropical air. Occasionally a small bulge of warm air pushes poleward into the cold air. The warm air flows upward over the cold air, creating an area of low pressure. Cold polar air flows into the low pressure area along a spiral path (because of the Earth's rotation). The winds speed up as they approach the center of the low; this increases the upward flow and the pressure drops even more. Soon the polar front has developed a much larger bulge. Along one edge of the bulge, warm air continues to rise over the cold air, forming a warm front. Along the other edge of the bulge, cold air moves under the warm air forming a cold front. The low pressure area, called a depression, is now fully developed and is blown eastward by the winds. But what goes up must come down. Soon a high pressure area develops nearby. Within the high pressure area, or anticyclone, air descends. This balances the upward flow of air from the depression. The anticyclones are blown eastward along with the depressions. So, the weather of these regions consists of a succession of anticyclones and depressions blown in from the west.

A low pressure area, or depression, over Europe. The direction of the winds can be deduced from Buys Ballot's law: if you stand with your back to the wind in the northern hemisphere, low pressure is to your left. Conversely, in the southern hemisphere, low pressure is to your right.

A typical frontal system associated with a northern hemisphere low pressure area or depression. A warm front moves anticlockwise around the low pressure center, followed by a cold front. Where the cold front has overtaken the warm front, an occluded front forms.

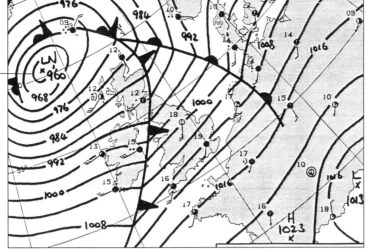

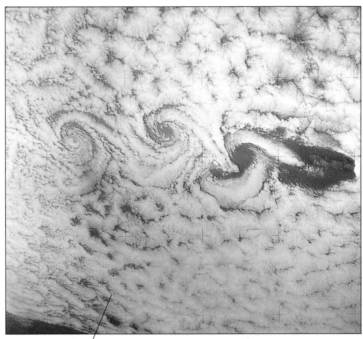

Cloud vortices over Baja California, Mexico. These turbulent conditions still manage to transport heat toward the poles, as is required if the weather machine is to work properly.

Admiral Francis Beaufort's notes on his wind speed scale for use at sea.

The jet stream

When high-flying aircraft first entered service, a surprising discovery was made. When flying westward across the Atlantic or across America, the aircraft were slowed down by powerful high-speed winds 6 miles (10km) up in the atmosphere. These eastward-blowing winds, traveling at hurricane speeds, were named the jet streams. The jet streams form at the polar front, where cold polar air meets warm tropical air. They are fast-moving rivers of air that blow at speeds between 200 and 400mph (322-644km/h). About 300 miles (480km) wide and four miles (6km) deep, the jet stream zig-zags around the world. Sometimes it may make three zig-zags during the course of its journey around the world; at other times, there may be four or five zig-zags. The jet streams have an important effect on the weather. If the stream flows from the north, it brings cold air from polar regions, and cold weather. Furthermore, where the stream moves toward the tropics, the air pressure tends to be higher than normal. Where the stream bends back toward the poles, air pressure tends to be low. Thus the jet stream encourages the formation of depressions where it turns northward, and anticyclones where it turns southward. Sometimes the jet stream can zig-zag so violently that a circular loop of wind is formed. These loops are called blocking highs. They bring extremes of weather, especially in northwest Europe. In 1990, a large blocking high was established over Europe for many months, causing an extended period of hot and dry weather.

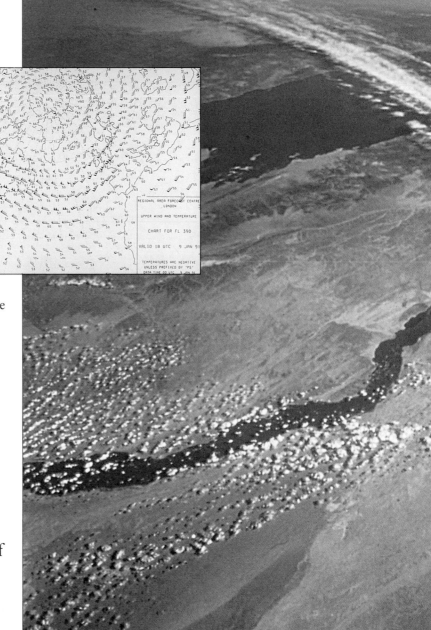

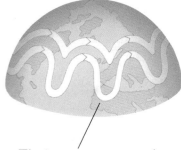

An upper wind and temperature forecast grid for the north Atlantic used to plan a transatlantic flight.

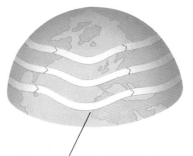

Jet streams in mid-latitudes follow a zig-zag path around the globe. The streams guide the paths of the low level weather systems.

The jet streams can wander north and south, forming larger undulations. This type of stream produces depressions in the lower atmosphere.

Gemini spacecraft photograph showing jet stream clouds over Egypt, in the foreground, and the Red Sea. The tip of the Sinai peninsula can be seen, jutting into the Red Sea, and the course of the River Nile is very clear.

❏ The fastest jet stream seen was found to be traveling at a speed of 408mph (656km/h) at a height of 154,200ft (47,000m) above South Uist, Outer Hebrides, Scotland.

❏ The jet streams blow from the west with such power that eastbound airliners fly across North America about one hour faster than airliners flying westward.

❏ A balloon released into the jet stream would take two weeks to travel completely around the globe.

During winter, in the northern hemisphere, the jet stream is strongest over the east coast of Asia, over the eastern U.S. and north Africa.

The undulations may develop into a stationary pattern of unconnected cells of high pressure called blocking highs, which produce settled weather.

Sheep and cattle are often moved between pens by means of 'either-or' gates. In the same way, bends in the jet stream can 'turn on and off' weather systems across the globe.

Small-scale weather

Local conditions influence the weather. A traveler from central New York State might leave home when there was a severe cold snap, with the local kids happily skating on the frozen ponds. In Boston, on the coast at the same latitude, the traveler might find the weather so mild that skating is impossible. This is because water both gains and loses heat more slowly than land does – the ocean still retains some of the warmth of summer in the depths of winter. Mountain ranges also influence local weather. Mountains can protect a locality, and act as a barrier to storms. The mighty Himalayas protect India from the cold air masses of north and central Asia, and so keep Indian winters mild. Mountains cause rain to fall when moist winds blow up their sides. The hot dry air produced after the rain falls means that the climate on the sheltered leeward side of mountains is often dry and parched. Local weather also depends upon the nature of the countryside. Sandy deserts, for example, absorb a high proportion of the Sun's energy. This is one of the reasons why deserts are so hot. Snow, on glaciers or mountain tops, absorbs only a small proportion of the Sun's energy, reflecting most back into the atmosphere. So icy areas tend to remain cold. In cities, the temperature is hotter than in the surrounding countryside. The roads and buildings absorb considerable heat. The city becomes a 'heat island.'

The Advanced Tactical Fighter is invisible to radar because it does not reflect radiation. In a similar way, forests and crops absorb the Sun's radiation and produce hot local climates.

Satellite image of New York, which stands out in blue. Large cities are warmer than their surroundings. They form 'heat islands.'

The Biosphere Project near Tucson, Arizona is a giant air- and water-tight glasshouse. It is an enclosed environment containing five ecosystems.

Eight people will spend two years inside the biosphere, along with 3,800 species of plants and animals. They will simulate living in a future space colony.

Mount McKinley in Alaska is the highest peak in North America. A permanent snowfield covers half the mountain, influencing the local climate.

The biosphere desert. The biosphere is divided into five completely self-sufficient 'biomes,' or microclimates. Each biome has its own plants and animals

Sand dunes in Death Valley, California. The dunes absorb about 65 percent of the radiation falling on them. This helps increase the temperature of the region.

❏ Living creatures create tiny weather systems called microclimates in their nests and burrows. For instance, bees fan their wings at the hive entrance during hot weather. This makes a cooling draft blow through the hive.

❏ New York city generates seven times more heat than it receives from the Sun. It is a classic example of a 'heat island.'

❏ In the northern hemisphere, a gentle south-facing slope can receive 50 percent extra heat at the beginning of January compared with level ground. As the year advances, and the Sun is higher in the sky, the advantage of sloping ground becomes less. In April the extra warmth may only amount to 15 percent.

❏ Wind barriers such as hedges give protection downwind for a distance of up to ten times the height of the barrier.

❏ The center of a large city can be as much as 9°F (5°C) hotter at night than the surrounding countryside. The bricks and concrete of the buildings and the pavement of the roads act like a giant storage heater, releasing during the night heat that was absorbed during the day.

Dew, fog, and smog

Radiation fog forms when the ground, and air close to it, cool rapidly at night.

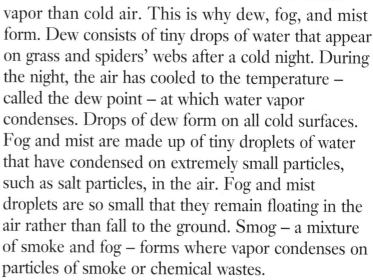

Humid days are uncomfortable, and 'muggy.' The cause of the problem is that humid air contains more water vapor than average. There is a limit to the amount of water vapor that air can hold at any particular temperature, so on a humid day our sweat is not able to evaporate from our skins and so cool us. The water vapor content of air is called its humidity. When expressed as a percentage of the maximum possible, it is called relative humidity. The relative humidity varies from 100 percent in clouds and fog to 10 percent or less in desert areas. Warm air can contain more water vapor than cold air. This is why dew, fog, and mist form. Dew consists of tiny drops of water that appear on grass and spiders' webs after a cold night. During the night, the air has cooled to the temperature – called the dew point – at which water vapor condenses. Drops of dew form on all cold surfaces. Fog and mist are made up of tiny droplets of water that have condensed on extremely small particles, such as salt particles, in the air. Fog and mist droplets are so small that they remain floating in the air rather than fall to the ground. Smog – a mixture of smoke and fog – forms where vapor condenses on particles of smoke or chemical wastes.

In industrial areas, smoke and chemical waste released into the air can cause smog.

In the fall, dew on a spider's web is a familiar sight after a cold night.

This village in the Canadian Arctic is enveloped in advection fog. This forms when a warm wind blows over the cold sea.

When damp air rises, it cools and clouds form. This forest high in the Andes Mountains is covered in almost perpetual mist.

This cyclist wears a mask to protect him from car exhaust fumes. On a foggy day pollution in the air can cause smog.

❏ 'Pea-souper' fogs of Victorian England got their name because they were colored yellow by industrial fumes, and hence thought to resemble the color of thick pea-soup. The worst 'pea-souper' occurred in December 1952. Around 4,000 people died from breathing problems associated with inhaling the fog.

❏ Fog is made up of tiny droplets between 1 and 10 microns across; mist droplets are even smaller, less than 1 micron. One micron equals 0.000039in (0.001mm), about 1/200th of the thickness of a human hair.

❏ Fogs over the seas on the Grand Banks, Newfoundland, Canada, can last for weeks on end. These are the longest-enduring fogs recorded in the world.

❏ According to an international definition, fog occurs when visibility is 600ft (180m) or less. Visibility in mist may extend up to 3,000ft (915m).

❏ Ice-fog – containing minute ice crystals – shines and glitters in sunlight. It is rather colorfully known as 'diamond dust.' Ice fogs frequently occur around Fairbanks, Alaska, where the temperature may drop to −40°F (−40°C) in winter.

Clouds – castles in the air

It is a warm summer day. Overhead a glider circles in the sky, looking for rising currents of air. The pilot knows that updrafts of air, called thermals, form over plowed fields and other warm areas. Over such places, bubbles of hot air form and then rise, like invisible hot air balloons. These updrafts do not only carry gliders upward; they also carry water vapor, and thus cause clouds to form. As air rises, it expands and cools. If the air cools enough, any water vapor in it will condense. Tiny droplets of liquid water, or perhaps small ice crystals, will form on microscopic particles of dust. A cloud will be born. The clouds formed by localized bubbles of rapidly-rising summer air are fleecy, 'cotton-wool' type. A glider pilot might find updrafts of air near mountains. As winds blow over mountains, they are forced to rise. Once again, the rising air will expand and cool. So, clouds and rain are often seen on the windward side of mountains and on mountain tops. Clouds also form along weather fronts, especially warm fronts. In these regions, large amounts of air are forced to rise by the gradual flow of air. The air flow may be slow, so that the air takes many hours to rise sufficiently for clouds to form. The clouds created in this way are widespread and sheet-like.

The cause of acid rain – fumes from the exhaust chimney of a power station. Modern power stations are fitted with equipment to remove sulfur dioxide from the fumes.

A column of warm air rises. Cloud forms as the air cools. When the column reaches a layer of colder air, the cloud spreads out.

Only about 40 percent of the energy consumed by burning coal in this power station will be transmitted as electricity. The remainder escapes into the atmosphere as waste heat.

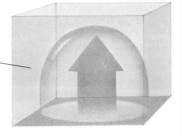

Clouds begin to form when a patch of warm ground heats the air above it. A bubble of warm air is created, resting on the ground.

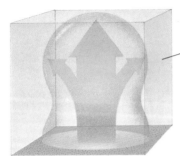

Because the bubble is warmer than the surrounding air, it rises like a hot air balloon. As the bubble rises, it expands and cools.

Early morning cloud fills a mountain valley. These clouds form like fog, by cooling during the night; they vanish when warmed by the morning Sun.

Eventually the rising air bubble cools to below dew point – the temperature below which water vapor condenses. The water vapor in the cooled air condenses on small particles of dust and salt. A cloud is formed and hangs in the air.

The water vapor rising from the cooling towers of a power station condenses to form fleecy, cumulus clouds. In the background, layered stratus clouds are seen in the sky.

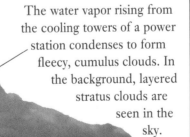

❑ The Pacific Ocean was explored by using clouds literally as 'landmarks.' Sailors found their way across the vast expanse of water by looking for the fleecy clouds that form above the islands. Once sighted, landfall could confidently be predicted.

❑ On average, about half of the sky worldwide is covered with cloud at any time. Satellites positioned in geostationary orbit 22,300 miles (35,880km) above the equator enable us to monitor global cloud cover with great accuracy.

❑ A small fluffy cloud may hold 100 to 1,000 tons (91 to 907 tonnes) of moisture. Looked at in another way, it is carrying around a weight of liquid equivalent to between 20 and 200 African elephants.

❑ Cloud droplets measure about 0.0008in (0.023mm) across, about one-fortieth of the size of a pinhead. They are so light that they float in the air.

Cloud types

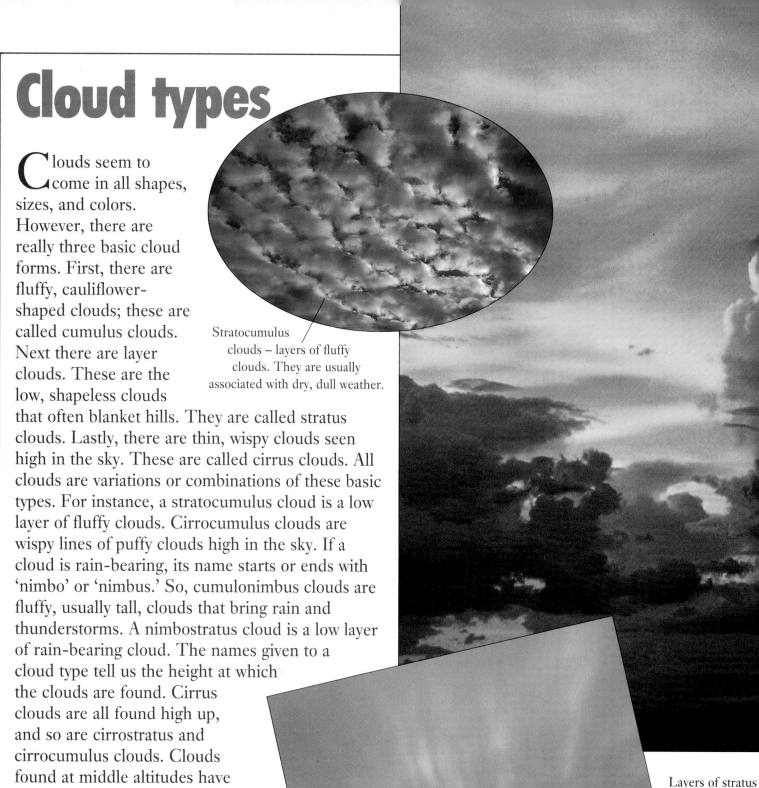

Clouds seem to come in all shapes, sizes, and colors. However, there are really three basic cloud forms. First, there are fluffy, cauliflower-shaped clouds; these are called cumulus clouds. Next there are layer clouds. These are the low, shapeless clouds that often blanket hills. They are called stratus clouds. Lastly, there are thin, wispy clouds seen high in the sky. These are called cirrus clouds. All clouds are variations or combinations of these basic types. For instance, a stratocumulus cloud is a low layer of fluffy clouds. Cirrocumulus clouds are wispy lines of puffy clouds high in the sky. If a cloud is rain-bearing, its name starts or ends with 'nimbo' or 'nimbus.' So, cumulonimbus clouds are fluffy, usually tall, clouds that bring rain and thunderstorms. A nimbostratus cloud is a low layer of rain-bearing cloud. The names given to a cloud type tell us the height at which the clouds are found. Cirrus clouds are all found high up, and so are cirrostratus and cirrocumulus clouds. Clouds found at middle altitudes have names beginning with 'alto.' There are two types of middle-height cloud: altostratus and altocumulus. Clouds found at lower levels are nimbostratus, stratocumulus and stratus. Cumulus and cumulonimbus clouds occur at a range of heights.

Stratocumulus clouds – layers of fluffy clouds. They are usually associated with dry, dull weather.

Layers of stratus clouds lying above pouch-like mammatus clouds. The mammatus clouds are associated with severe thunderstorms and windy weather.

Thundercloud over Tucson, Arizona. Thunderclouds are called cumulonimbus clouds. The upper parts often spread out in the form of a large anvil, called the thunderhead.

Cumulus clouds over Santa Rosa, New Mexico. Cumulus clouds are associated with sunny weather.

❏ The highest ordinary type of cloud is the cirrus, which occurs at an average altitude of 27,000ft (8,250m). These clouds contain extremely cold water at −31°F (−35°C).

❏ A cumulonimbus cloud can be enormous: six miles (10km) across and eleven miles (18km) high, twice as high as Mount Everest.

❏ The winds inside cumulonimbus clouds may reach speeds of 124mph (200km/h), as fast as many express trains.

❏ The system used today of naming clouds according to their shape and height was devised in 1803 by a London druggist and amateur weather-watcher, Luke Howard.

❏ Pink mother-of-pearl clouds may be found at heights of 80,000ft (24,000m). These clouds are very thin and can usually only be seen for a short time before sunrise or after sunset, when the sky is dark. The clouds are lit by the Sun which is below the horizon.

Rain – nature's bounty

Cloud droplets are small and light. Most of them float in the air, like mist, without falling. However, some droplets may be slightly heavier. These heavier droplets start to fall and, as they fall, they collide with other droplets, coalescing to form bigger drops. The large drops eventually fall as rain. Within shallow clouds, the droplets may not increase much in size before they hit the ground; the fine rain produced is called drizzle. Inside large clouds, such as cumulonimbus clouds, falling droplets have further to fall, so they can grow into larger drops. Heavier rain falls from these clouds. In cold regions, where the tops of clouds often contain ice crystals, rain forms by another process. Here, ice crystals fall and grow large by coalescence. In the lower parts of the cloud, the ice crystals melt, and continue their fall as raindrops. Steady rain is produced where a continuous flow of moist warm air is forced to rise. This happens at warm fronts where warm air flows over a mass of cold air. As long as the flow of warm moist air continues, rain will fall. In a cold front, where cold air flows under a warm air mass, the rain is short-lived. Rain falls as the warm air at the front is forced upward but stops when the front is passed.

A hole in cloud produced by a 'seeding' experiment. Silver iodide or salt crystals are dropped from an airplane to make water particles condense and fall as rain.

Enough rain falls each year to give every person in the U.S. 900 baths a day.

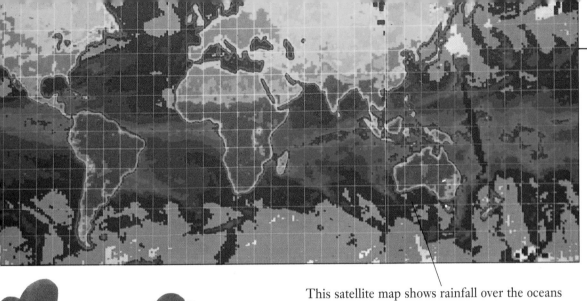

This satellite map shows rainfall over the oceans during January 12-16, 1973. The dark blue areas are drier than the light blue. Black represents dry regions with no cloud or low humidity. Light grey indicates dry Arctic air.

Dark cumulonimbus clouds tower up into the sky from a flat base. They bring heavy rain, often accompanied by thunder and lightning.

❑ Every minute of the day 1,000 million tons (907 million tonnes) of water fall as rain around the world. Each raindrop is made up of several million cloud droplets. The average rainfall around the world is 40in (1,016mm) per year.

❑ We may colloquially refer to a heavy downpour as 'raining cats and dogs,' but in 1881 crabs and periwinkles fell as rain into the streets of Worcester, England. They had been carried from the sea 40 miles (64km) away by a violent storm before being deposited on the unwary townspeople. 'A hard rain' indeed!

❑ In 1755, rain the color of blood fell in Locarno, Switzerland. The color was caused by red dust carried from the Sahara desert over 1,850 miles (3,000km) by the wind.

❑ If all the water in the atmosphere at any one time was to fall as rain, it would cover the entire Earth's surface to a depth of 1in (2.5cm).

Acid rain – a cocktail of chemicals

A young man walks through a forest in southern Norway. He reflects that the forest has changed since he played among its trees and swam in the nearby lake as a child. Many of the spruce trees have died. The crowns of the remaining trees have thinned. The needles have turned brown. The water of the lake is unnaturally clear. There is a green carpet of algae and moss in the lake, but no fish. These are the effects of acid rain. The cause of the trouble lies far away, in the industrial cities, perhaps cities in other countries. Air pollution can travel great distances.

Acid rain damages stone that contains calcium carbonate, such as limestone. This lion is pitted with holes caused by acid rain.

The chief culprit in this case is sulfur dioxide, a chemical produced when coal and oil are burnt. Once sulfur dioxide reaches the air, it combines with water droplets to form an acid. When the droplets fall as rain, the rain is acid enough slowly to kill forests and fish in lakes. Another culprit is nitrogen oxide, given off by power stations and automobile exhausts, which also quickly changes to acid in the air. These gases, and other industrial pollutants, turn the air into a dangerous cocktail of chemicals that destroys the fabric of buildings, as well as forests and lakes.

Power stations burn large amounts of coal and oil. Tall chimneys reduce local pollution, but do not prevent sulfur dioxide from entering the atmosphere.

Many modern cars now have catalytic converters that reduce the output of harmful exhaust gases. In some countries, they are required by law.

The damage caused to trees by acid rain is shown in their growth rings. The outer layers of growth will be less vigorous than the inner ones. Large areas of forest in northeast U.S.A. and northern Europe are now dying.

This satellite map shows sulfur dioxide released by the volcano Mount Pinatubo in the Philippines in June 1991. The highest concentrations of gas are shown as white. They are centered over the Bay of Bengal.

These trees in the Appalachian Mountains have been killed by acid rain.

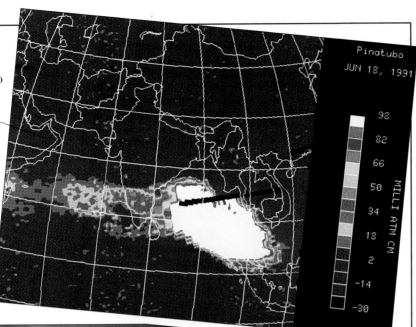

Pinatubo
JUN 18, 1991

98
82
66
50
34
18
2
-14
-30

MILLI ATM CM

❏ Rain fell in Scotland in 1974 that was nearly as acidic as lemon juice. Smog in Los Angeles has been measured to be more acidic than lemon juice. Rain in New York State is often ten times more acidic than unpolluted rain.

❏ An estimated 165 million tons (150 million tonnes) of sulfur dioxide were released into the atmosphere by burning fossil fuels in 1989.

❏ In Britain about two-thirds of all trees are damaged by acid rain, although the effects are not as obvious as they are in Czechoslovakia and Germany.

❏ Many countries produce little sulfur dioxide but receive large amounts as pollution from their neighbors. Norway, for example, receives over five times more sulfur dioxide than it emits. It is thought that most of the pollution comes from Britain, borne on westerly breezes. Acid rain falling on Alaska is thought to originate in Japan.

❏ The amount of ozone, a type of oxygen that helps form acid rain, in the lower atmosphere has doubled over Europe in the last thirty years. In other parts of the world, ozone in the atmosphere has decreased. There is an 'ozone hole' over the Antarctic where ozone has disappeared completely from the upper atmosphere.

The Bible story tells how, after the Flood, Noah released a dove to search for land.

Flood – water in turmoil

Too much water in too small a space, or in too short a time, brings flood and disaster. Most spectacular are flash floods, which occur very suddenly and with little warning. Until 1972, the residents of Calama, in Chile, probably thought they were immune from floods. They lived in the Atacama desert in the rain shadow of the Andes mountain range. There had been no rain for 400 years. Nevertheless, in the mid-afternoon of February 10, 1972, torrential rain fell, causing devastating floods and landslides. In 1976, in Big Thompson Canyon, Colorado, 10in (250mm) of rain fell over the mountains at the end of the canyon in 4 hours. The resulting flood waters surged down from the mountains, leaving a 15-mile (24-km) wide trail of devastation across the countryside. Eighty people were killed. Widespread floods are caused when river banks burst after periods of heavy rainfall. In July 1991, 1,700 people were killed and 2 million made homeless in China by the rising waters of the Chang (Yangtze), a river with a long history of disastrous floods. The river rose to more than 3ft (1m) above the danger line. High tides pushed the river level even higher near the coast. High incoming tides and down-river floods, such as occurred on this occasion, are a lethal combination for towns near the mouths of rivers.

This stained glass window in Canterbury Cathedral, England, tells the story of Noah's Flood.

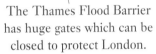

The Thames Flood Barrier has huge gates which can be closed to protect London.

Monsoons regularly flood the plains of India. Crops may be ruined and lives lost.

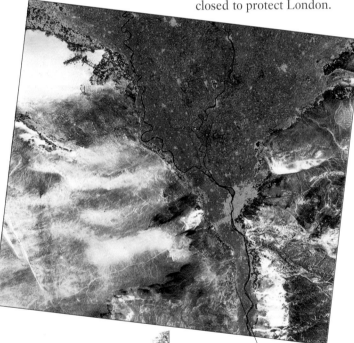

This satellite photograph shows the delta of the river Nile. The area used to suffer from annual flooding, but now the Aswan Dam controls the floods and allows year-round irrigation.

Floods happen when a river cannot carry away all the water entering it. This picture shows several streets in Saarburg, Germany, under water.

❑ Noah's Flood, mentioned in the Bible, was probably one of many that inundated the Tigris-Euphrates region of present-day Iraq around 4000 B.C. Excavations at the ancient city of Ur have revealed a layer of mud from the Flood.

❑ In July 1991 nearly 11in (280mm) of rain fell in the Osan-Suwon area, south of Seoul, South Korea, in less than four hours. The floods caused by the rains were the worst for over 25 years.

❑ In November 1970, 1 million people lost their lives when a hurricane struck the Ganges Delta Islands in Bangladesh, causing widespread flooding. Less than half of the 1.4 million population of the four islands of Bhola, Charjabbar, Hatia, and Ramagati survived.

❑ London experienced its worst rainstorm in August 1975 when almost 7in (178mm) of rain fell in about three hours. The resulting flood waters carried cars down the streets and burst sewers. The shower was localized; a short distance from the center of the storm, there was practically no rain.

❑ The counterpart of Noah in Greek mythology is Deucalion. When the god Zeus, angry with mankind, caused a great deluge to destroy the human race, Deucalion built an ark to save himself and his wife, Pyrrha. After ten days of rain, it came safely to rest upon Mount Parnassus.

Drought – the parched Earth

The latest research into the cause of droughts seems to show that the oceans have a greater effect on our weather than was previously thought. There appears to be a definite link between sea temperatures and the amount of rain falling. For example, it has been found that when the south Atlantic seas are unusually warm during spring, there is a summer drought in the Sahel of Africa – a wide belt of land south of the Sahara. The reason seems to be that air pressure is reduced over warm seas and this causes a reduction in the southwesterly winds that normally bring rain to west Africa and the Sahel. Scientists also suspect that a warm ocean current in the Pacific is linked with droughts in various parts of the world. The current is called El Niño – the Christ Child – because it only flows around Christmas time. El Niño starts just north of Papua New Guinea and flows eastward across the Pacific toward Ecuador, then turning southward along the coast of Peru. It is irregular, occurring once every three to eight years. When El Niño does flow, it seems to have a powerful effect on the weather around the world. It flowed in 1982-3, and the next year 1983 was exceptionally warm with milder than normal winters in the United States. Similarly, El Niño flowed in 1986-7, and was followed by the exceptionally hot and dry years of 1987-90.

Too little rain causes crops to fail. No plants will grow in this soil, which has baked hard in the sun and cracked from lack of rain.

Soil erosion in the Valley of the Moon of the Atacama Desert, Chile. In some parts of the Atacama Desert, rain has never been recorded.

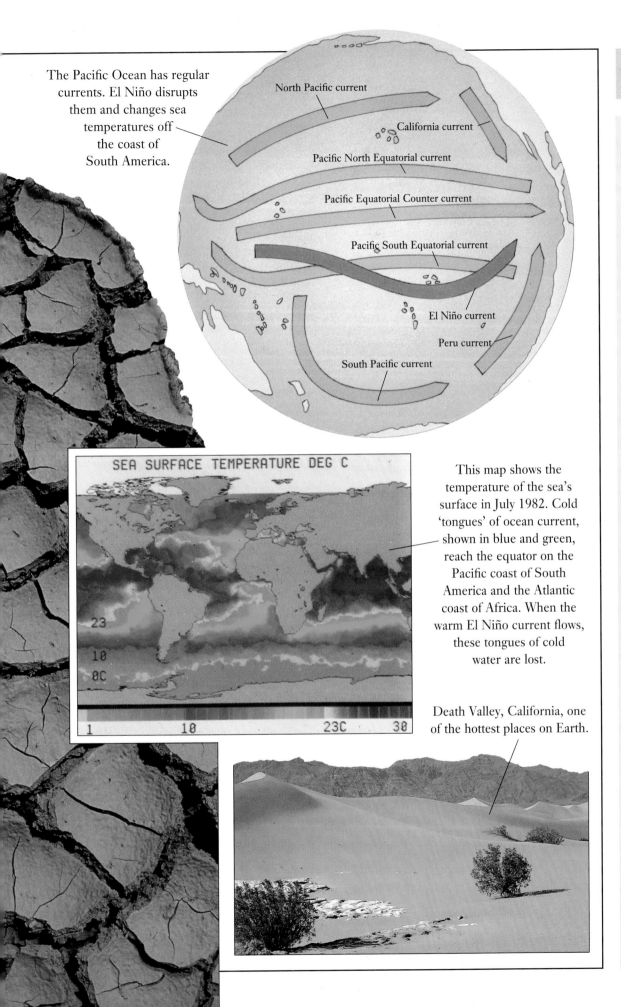

The Pacific Ocean has regular currents. El Niño disrupts them and changes sea temperatures off the coast of South America.

North Pacific current

California current

Pacific North Equatorial current

Pacific Equatorial Counter current

Pacific South Equatorial current

El Niño current

Peru current

South Pacific current

SEA SURFACE TEMPERATURE DEG C

23

18

8C

1   18   23C   38

This map shows the temperature of the sea's surface in July 1982. Cold 'tongues' of ocean current, shown in blue and green, reach the equator on the Pacific coast of South America and the Atlantic coast of Africa. When the warm El Niño current flows, these tongues of cold water are lost.

Death Valley, California, one of the hottest places on Earth.

Hail – frozen rain

Hailstones develop when small droplets of frozen rain form high in a thundercloud – about 6 miles (10km) above ground level, where the temperature is freezing. The small pellets of ice initially drop downward, but are then caught in updrafts within the turbulent storm cloud. They are carried back to the freezing part of the cloud, and more ice freezes around them. Again they drop downward, and the process is repeated. Each time the ice particle is tossed up and down within the cloud, it gains a layer of ice. Eventually it becomes heavy enough to fall to the ground. In 1930, five German glider pilots experienced the conditions inside a thundercloud at close quarters, with tragic results. Caught in the thundercloud over the Rhön mountains, they bailed out. They were carried up and down within the cloud, becoming coated with ice as hailstones do, until they fell to the ground, trapped within an ice prison. Only one man survived the ordeal. On rare occasions, large lumps of ice, called ice meteors, fall from the sky. An ice meteor weighing 4.4lb (2kg) fell at Cordoba, Spain in 1829. The cause of these falling ice chunks is unknown. Some may be ice falling from passing aircraft, or perhaps they are super hailstones, carried aloft by very strong updrafts.

Hailstones are usually 0.2-2in (5-50mm) in diameter. A stone over 0.4in (10mm) is larger than average. One over 2in (50mm) may be several smaller stones frozen together.

This polarized light photograph (right) shows the internal crystal structure of a very large hailstone. The rings are built up rather like the growth rings of a tree trunk (above).

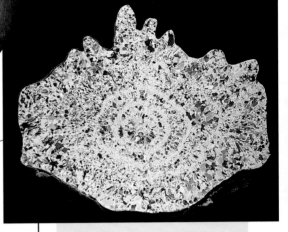

One of the most violent hailstorms of recent times was in Munich, Germany on July 12, 1984. Stones as large as 2in (50mm) plummeted down, smashing roof tiles.

A hail cloud. Large hailstones are often made up of alternate layers of clear and white ice. If the temperature inside a cloud is very low the ice freezes rapidly and is clear. The ice is white if it is slightly warmer.

❏ The largest hailstone found in the United States fell at Coffeyville, Kansas, on September 3, 1970. It weighed 1.67lb (758g) and measured 17.5in (445mm) around, the size of a melon.

❏ Fossilized imprints of ancient hailstones have been found preserved in rocks from about 160 million years ago discovered in Yorkshire, U.K.

❏ Ice stones weighing over 3lb (1.4kg) fell around Messina, Italy, in 1857. Fishermen in an open boat survived by jumping overboard and sheltering under the hull of their vessel.

❏ On June 16, 1882, at Dubuque, Iowa, two frogs were found frozen inside hailstones. A turtle was found inside a hailstone the size of a brick that fell near Vicksburg, Mississippi, in 1984.

❏ On April 14, 1986, hailstones weighing up to 2.25lb (1.02kg) fell in the Gopalganji district of Bangladesh, killing 92 people.

Ice – solid water

Ice is solid water. It forms when water freezes. Since water is a unique substance with some surprising properties, we can be sure that ice will surprise us too. For instance, did you know that ice can wear down mountains? The process is called weathering and occurs because water expands when it freezes to form ice. When water in a crack in a mountain top rock freezes, the expanded ice forces the rock apart, perhaps splitting it. The expansion can create enormous forces – a force of 200lb (90kg) on each square inch (6.5cm^2), equivalent to the weight of three elephants on an area the size of a dinner plate. This force cracks the rock, gradually breaking it down to smaller and smaller pieces. Eventually pieces are blown away by the wind. Another surprise is that, in polar regions, where the temperature can reach −40°F (−40°C), water poured on to the ground takes a few moments to freeze. This is because every time a little of the water freezes, some latent heat is released, helping to delay the solidification of the rest. However, if water is thrown into the air, it freezes immediately, exploding into a dazzling shower of ice crystals with an audible hiss. This is because the water is split up into a cloud of small droplets when thrown, and the heat released does not spread amongst the other minute droplets of water.

Freak weather conditions can cause enormous damage to crops. Very low temperatures near Tampa, Florida, have caused icicles to form on this citrus tree.

When the atmosphere is full of frosty fog, water vapor in the air will crystallize on any rough surface. These 'flowers' of hoar frost have formed on a scratched window pane.

This photograph of an ice stalactite was taken using polarized light. The ice appears to have colors in it. This happens because the outer layers freeze before the inner part, causing stress in the crystal structure. Liquid water appears colorless under polarized light.

This stone split when water in a crack froze.

If the temperature drops below freezing at night, small ice crystals form on blades of grass and fallen leaves as frost.

❏ About 89 percent of the ice on Earth is contained in the Antarctic ice sheet. The average depth of the surface ice sheet in Antarctica is 4,920ft (1,500m).

❏ Permafrost (subsoil that is permanently frozen) may reach almost 45,000ft (13,700m) below ground level. The deepest frosts have been found in Siberia, eastern Russia.

❏ On January 6, 1979, a huge ice floe broke loose on Vladivostok Bay, Russia, carrying nearly 3,000 people who had been fishing on the ice out to sea. Twenty ships and three helicopters were needed to rescue them.

❏ River ice forms first on the inner parts of curved banks where the flow is slowest. Ice forms least readily where the water speeds up, such as when flowing around islands.

❏ Weathering of rocks and mountains is a very slow process. A mountain is worn down by 3in (90mm) every 1,000 years. At this rate, the Empire State Building would take over 4 million years to wear away.

❏ Greenland is covered with an ice cap up to 14,000ft (4,300m) thick; so inhospitable is the climate here, that less than 5 percent of the island is inhabitable.

Snow – winter's white blanket

Snow crystals form inside very cold clouds. The ice crystals form on tiny dust particles in the cloud. The crystals grow in size as more and more ice builds up on them. When the crystals become heavy they drop down through the clouds. If the temperature is cold enough, the crystals remain frozen until they reach the ground. There are several different crystal shapes. In high clouds, the crystals are shaped like six-sided hexagonal needles; in middle-height clouds, the crystals may have either a needle or a flat six-sided plate shape. In low clouds, snow crystals form in a wide variety of shapes, although they are always six-sided. The different crystal shapes reflect the fact that water molecules – the smallest particles of water – are V-shaped. When the molecules join together during freezing, there are a large number of ways that the V-shaped molecules can link together, and so many different crystal shapes are possible. However, the angle between the arms of the V is such that they always form into six-sided units. Usually, snow does not fall as single crystals, but as flakes formed when crystals coalesce and freeze together. It is said that no identical snow flakes have ever been found. However, most flakes exhibit the six-sided shape of the crystals from which they are built.

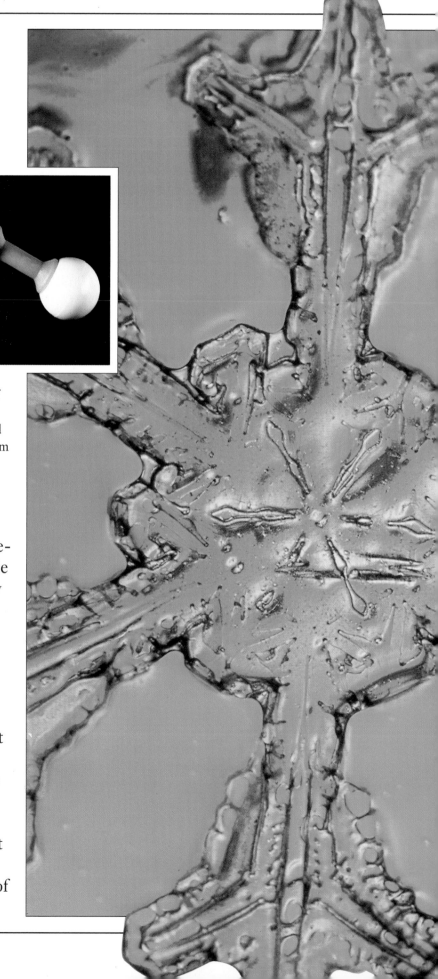

This model of a molecule of water shows two atoms of hydrogen making a V-shaped angle of 105° with a single atom of oxygen.

Although Mount Kilimanjaro in Africa lies close to the equator, the peaks are snow-capped throughout the year. The mountain is so high that more snow falls than is lost through melting and evaporation.

This micro-photograph of a snowflake shows the hexagonal center from which six branches form as the crystal grows. Each crystal is made from V-shaped water molecules, which are linked together in different ways.

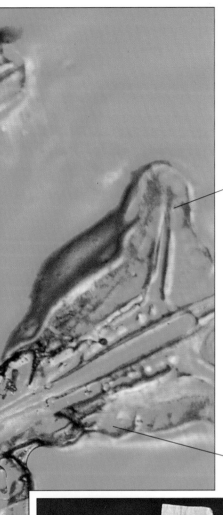

No two snow crystals are identical because their formation is influenced by temperature, humidity, air currents, and other factors. These conditions are different for every individual crystal.

An iceberg is a mass of land ice that has broken off or 'calved' from a glacier or ice sheet.

Snowflakes always have six points, but each pattern is unique.

Thunder and lightning

A boy's hair standing on end during a science lesson demonstration. His hair has been charged with static electricity.

An artist's impression of ball lightning. Ball lightning is a round glowing object that floats in the air. The ball – up to 3ft (1m) across – may move around and then explode.

Inside a thunder cloud, currents of air carry water droplets and hailstones upward. As the hailstones and water droplets travel upward they rub against one another. This gives them a charge of static electricity in the same way that a plastic comb becomes charged with electricity when it is quickly pulled through your hair. After a while, large amounts of static electricity build up in the cloud. There is a concentration of charge at the top of the cloud, carried there by light particles and droplets lifted by the upcurrents of air. The bottom of the cloud also becomes charged because heavier particles and droplets tend to fall to the lower layers of the cloud. After a while, there may be a giant spark – a lightning flash – as electricity jumps between the bottom and the top of the cloud. This sort of lightning is called sheet lightning because it is often hidden from direct view and is seen as a flickering light inside the cloud. The lightning heats the air along its path to a very high temperature. This causes an immense clap of thunder as the heated air expands outward at great speed. Sometimes lightning will jump between the bottom of a cloud and the ground. This is called forked lightning.

Lightning results when large electric charges build up in a thundercloud. A surge of electricity flows upward from the ground to neutralize the charge.

The temperature inside the main lightning stroke can reach 54,000°F (30,000°C), five times hotter than the surface of the Sun.

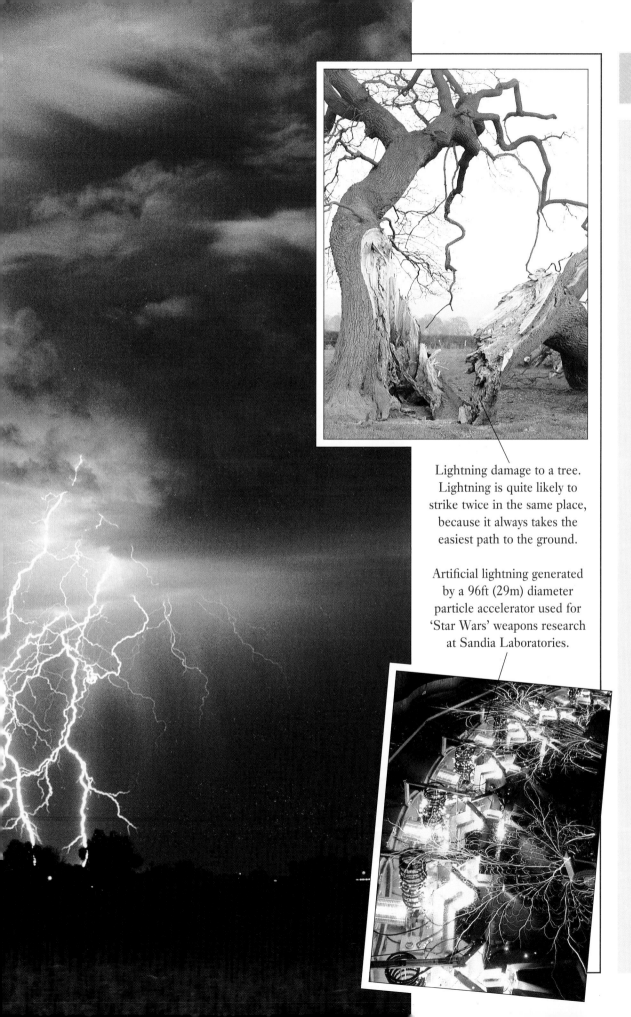

Lightning damage to a tree. Lightning is quite likely to strike twice in the same place, because it always takes the easiest path to the ground.

Artificial lightning generated by a 96ft (29m) diameter particle accelerator used for 'Star Wars' weapons research at Sandia Laboratories.

❏ Every year there are more than 16 million thunder storms around the world – an average of 45,000 a day. At any time, there are 2,000 in progress.

❏ Thunder can be usually heard 10 miles (16km) away, but it has been heard from over 40 miles (65km) away.

❏ A summer thunder storm releases as much energy as a dozen Hiroshima-type atomic bombs exploding simultaneously. This is equivalent to the explosion of 240,000 tons of TNT.

❏ A lightning flash lasts only a tiny fraction of a second; persistence of the image in our eyes after the lightning has in reality disappeared makes it appear longer.

❏ The downward or leader stroke of a lightning flash can travel at speeds of over 1,000 miles/sec (1,600km/sec). The main upward flash is much faster, up to 87,000 miles/sec (140,000km/sec) which is nearly half the speed of light.

❏ In 1975, the umpire of a cricket match near Berwick-upon-Tweed in England was struck by lightning; he survived the experience, but it welded solid an iron joint in his leg.

❏ The central core of a lightning flash may only be 0.5in (12.7mm) across. The core is surrounded by a glowing region up to 20ft (6m) across.

Weather science – the early days

The science of weather prediction began when accurate instruments for measuring temperature, air pressure, humidity, wind direction and speed were developed. In 1593, the great Italian scientist Galileo Galilei made the first thermometer. It consisted of a thin glass tube 18in (46cm) long standing upright in a bowl of water. As the temperature varied, the water level in the tube went up and down. A crude thermometer indeed, but later scientists improved the design. In 1714, the German Gabriel Fahrenheit, introduced a temperature scale with 180 degrees between the freezing (32°F) and boiling temperatures (212°F) of water. Anders Celsius, a Swedish astronomer, introduced his scale, with 100 degrees between the freezing and boiling temperatures of water, in 1742. The first barometer was made in 1643 by a pupil of Galileo, called Evangelista Torricelli. It consisted of a mercury-filled tube, standing upright in a pool of mercury. Blaise Pascal, a French mathematician, showed the link between the height of the mercury in Torricelli's barometer and air pressure by a simple experiment. He persuaded his younger brother to carry a Torricelli barometer to the summit of a mountain, 3,458ft (1,054m) above sea level. The level of mercury fell by 3.33in (84mm) during the climb.

A sunshine recorder, or parheliometer. It focuses the Sun's rays to burn a line on heat-sensitive paper.

An early sunshine recorder. This type of recorder, using a glass ball, was first made by Irish scientist George Stokes. The Sun's rays are focused on the inner walls of the device, making a small burn mark.

An 1880 barograph, a barometer that automatically records air pressure. As the air pressure changes, a pen moves up and down on a rotating sheet of paper.

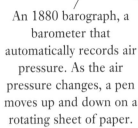

Official temperatures are recorded by a thermometer in a white box, called a Stevenson screen.

An early air thermometer, made by Robert Fludd (1574-1637), drawn within a circle which represents the universe.

The deployment of a weather buoy. A buoy is carried along by the ocean currents and transmits observations via satellites.

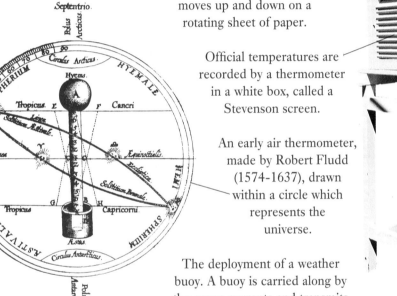

ODAS 21 G

FACT FILE

❏ Swedish scientist, Anders Celsius, the originator in 1742 of the centigrade temperature scale, invented his scale 'wrong way round.' He made the boiling point of water 0° and the freezing point of water 100°. Other scientists quickly realized that the scale was more convenient if it was reversed.

❏ In 1646, Athanasius Kircher, a professor of mathematics and Hebrew in Rome, first suggested that a solid ball of glass might be used to burn a mark on paper or wood to record the hours of sunlight. It was not until 1853 that the idea was applied. Scotsman John Francis Campbell used a spherical bowl of water to produce a scorch mark on wood as a recording of the hours of sunlight. In 1875, Irish scientist and mathematician George Stokes improved Campbell's instrument by using a solid glass ball as the lens to concentrate the Sun's rays.

❏ Kew observatory in London was one of the first to be equipped with a sunshine recorder in 1880. Sunshine records were kept for 100 years until the observatory was closed in 1980.

❏ A continuous set of weather records have been kept at the Radcliffe Observatory, Oxford, England since 1815.

Forecasting the weather

By the late 1700s, the instruments needed to make accurate forecasts had been developed. There was, however, a vital element missing: a method of quickly gathering information from widely separated places. No accurate forecast can be made from local observations only. And, of course, a forecast is of little use if the news can be transmitted no faster than a stage coach or ship can travel. The missing element was provided by the electromagnetic telegraph invented by American Samuel Morse in 1837. The usefulness of the new instrument was immediately grasped by Joseph Henry, secretary of the Smithsonian Institution in Washington, D.C. He organized a network of observers who telegraphed weather data to Washington each morning.

Weather maps were published each day although, strictly speaking, the maps were not forecasts. In Europe, the new technology was first put to use by the French. In 1854, during the Crimean War, French and English warships had been destroyed by a surprise storm at Balaclava. The lesson was quickly learnt. Two years later the French set up the first telegraphic weather forecasting system. By 1863, regular weather maps and forecasts for Europe were published. Rapid communications is still a vital component of weather services. The modern equivalent of the telegraph system is the Global Telecommunications System – a network of telephone, telex, and satellite links that join weather bureaus around the world.

Drawing a weather chart. Weather charts show the air pressure, wind speed and direction, cloud cover, temperature, and humidity. They are used to make short-term weather forecasts.

American inventor and artist Samuel Morse (1791-1872) invented the telegraph in 1837. It was soon used by meteorologists to gather weather data from over wide areas.

Radar map of a storm. Radar not only locates rain, snow, and hail; the strength of the signal reflected by the storm clouds shows how heavy the rain is, and the direction of winds driving it.

Telecommunications tower. Every minute of the day, weather data is being transmitted to weather centers worldwide.

A radar system used to detect rain, hail, and snow. It works by bouncing radio signals off rainfall.

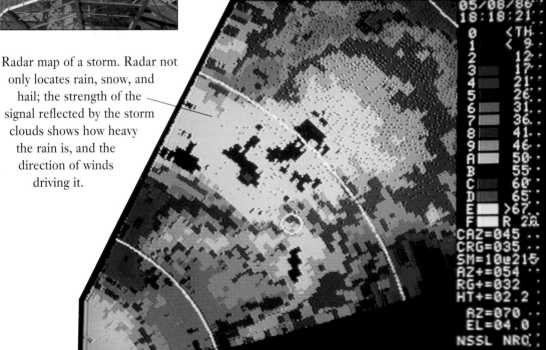

Eye in the sky

Modern weather forecasting depends upon a formidable array of high-tech instruments, which are constantly observing the weather and atmospheric conditions, and relaying information back to weather centers. Conditions on the ground are monitored by a network of 10,000 permanent weather stations around the world. Information is also gathered by weather buoys floating on the sea and by weather ships. Information on conditions in the upper atmosphere is gathered by radar, aircraft, satellites, balloons, and rockets. Radar can detect rain up to several hundred miles away. Specially-fitted weather aircraft fitted with sophisticated instruments make regular flights to monitor conditions. Commercial aircraft automatically report weather conditions along their flight paths. Balloons carry packets of instruments to heights of 20-25 miles (35-40km), transmitting data as they rise. High in the sky, weather satellites keep constant watch. There are two types of satellite: polar satellites and geostationary satellites. Polar satellites circle the Earth from pole to pole. They orbit the world in about 100 minutes at a height of around 530 miles (850km). Geostationary satellites stay in a fixed position 22,300 miles (35,880km) above the equator because their orbital speed exactly matches the speed of the Earth's rotation beneath them. From this vantage point, the satellite observes a wide area of the Earth's surface.

The ITOS-1 weather satellite orbited 900 miles (1,440km) above the Earth in the 1970s. The satellite is seen making a nighttime scan of cloud cover using infrared sensors.

Blue areas are San Francisco city suburbs. To the south, the two lakes mark the infamous San Andreas Fault.

A clear day over San Francisco. The all-seeing eye of the Landsat satellite reveals minute details of the world below.

Computer-colored image of the Earth from the European Meteosat weather satellite. Land is shown in brown, ocean in blue, cloud in yellow.

A balloon carrying weather instruments lifts off.

This hammer acts rather like a geostationary satellite. As the thrower spins to build up speed, the hammer stays in the same position relative to him as he turns.

Forecasting by numbers

Scientists studying a plot of the seasonal changes of ozone in the atmosphere. Computer analysis has revealed the damage done by pollution.

Computer-generated map of the world showing the average amount of cloud for January and July. Tropical areas and the Sahara (red, orange, and yellow) have less cloud than temperate areas (green).

Thousands of weather observations are made each day all over the world. The information gathered is passed, through the Global Communications System, to the world's major forecasting centers at Washington D.C. and Bracknell, England. Here, powerful computers carry out calculations and produce a 'numerical weather prediction.' These predictions are the basis of modern forecasting. To make a computer forecast, the area of the forecast is divided into a series of horizontal locations, called gridpoints. Above the gridpoints, the atmosphere is divided into a series of vertical levels. The next step is to analyze the data received from around the world, to derive the pressure, wind, temperature, and humidity at each gridpoint at a particular time. Once this is done, the derived values are taken as the starting points of the computer calculation. Using the laws of physics and mathematics, the computer calculates how the pressure, wind, temperature, and humidity will change at each gridpoint during a short period, called the time-step. For an accurate forecast, gridpoints should be at most about 60 miles (100km) apart, with 20 vertical levels. For a world-wide forecast, there would be about 60,000 gridpoints. With so many gridpoints, about 10 million numbers are needed to describe the state of the atmosphere at any time. Using a time-step of 10 minutes, about 1,500 million calculations are needed to produce a daily global weather forecast. It is no wonder that powerful computers are needed to do this.

CLOUD AMOUNT

JANUARY 1984   GLOBAL MONTHLY MEAN = 60

JULY 1984   GLOBAL MONTHLY MEAN = 62

SOURCE: ISCCP/ROSSOW   NASA/GISS

0   10   20   30   40   50   60   70   80   90   100
PERCENT

The computers used to study weather have revealed hidden beauty in mathematical data. This picture, called a fractal image, was made by a computer.

❑ Englishman Lewis Richardson was the first person to try calculating the weather using mathematical equations. He estimated that he would need 64,000 people working 24 hours a day, every day of the year, to perform all the arithmetic needed for a regular daily forecast.

❑ An early computer used for weather forecasting was called MANIAC, or the Mathematical Analyzer, Numerator, Integrator, And Computer. It was built by John von Neumann, a Hungarian-American mathematician at Princeton University, New Jersey. During the first trials, the computer often lived up to its name. It took 10 years of research before reasonable forecasts of weather patterns were obtained from the computer.

❑ The two largest weather computers are in Washington, D.C., and Bracknell, England. These computers can perform at very high speeds – about 3,000 million calculations per second.

❑ A global 24-hour forecast with 20 levels and 62-mile (100-km) grid spacing takes about 7 minutes to calculate. This is a short time compared to the several hours needed to analyze the raw data received from around the world upon which it is based.

Meteorologists surrounded by banks of visual-display units and computer equipment used for weather forecasting. The computer calculates the behavior of a simplified 'model' of the atmosphere.

A modern supercomputer. These ultra-powerful computers are used in major weather centers around the globe.

Looking back – discovering climates of the past

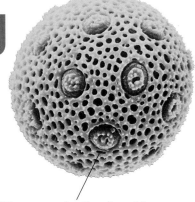

Every year a tree grows a new ring, or growth layer, around its trunk. If the weather has been warm and moist, the tree will grow well and the growth ring will be wide. A bad, cold year produces a thin growth ring. So, by looking at the growth rings in trees, scientists can learn about the weather of the past. Clues about past climates can be found in the polar ice caps, too. If a drill hole is made deep into the ice, a long core of ice can be pulled out. Distinct layers of ice can be seen. Tiny bubbles of gas frozen in each layer can be analyzed chemically to reveal what the atmosphere was like when each layer of ice froze. This reveals the temperature at the time, since some gases are more likely to be found in hot climates. Other clues to the past include microscopic pollen grains found fossilized in old rock layers. Some plants thrive in hot climates, other in cold climates. By seeing which plants left pollen in rocks of a known age, scientists have a rough guide to past climates. From these clues, it is clear that the Earth's climate changes slowly over the centuries. Warm periods are followed by periods of intense cold, when ice covers much of the Earth. These times are called ice ages.

The types of pollen found in a fossil reveal what plants lived long ago. These red campion pollen grains are magnified over 400 times.

The annual growth rings of trees record years of climate change. They reveal information about which years were wet and good for tree growth.

An ice core is cut into sections for sampling. A portion of each section is melted and a sample of the water is chemically analyzed. This gives information about climate changes in Antarctica.

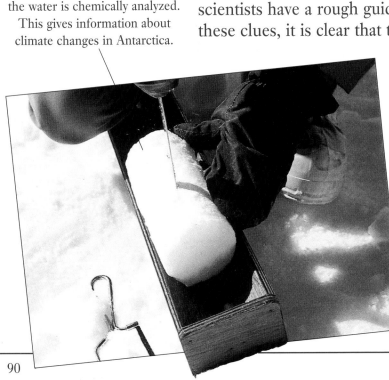

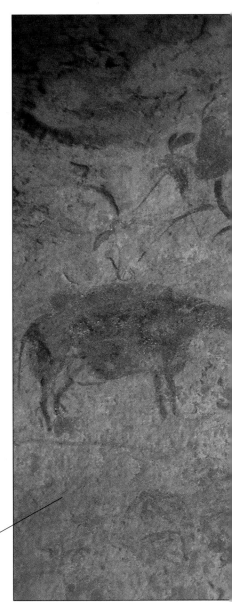

The animals shown in primitive cave paintings give important clues about the climate in prehistoric times.

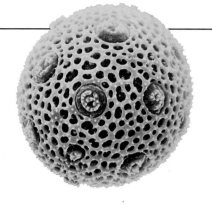

Glaciers cover 6 million square miles (15 million km²) of the Earth's surface. During ice ages, they extended much further. Rocks left behind when glaciers melted have been found in India, Australia, and South Africa.

❏ Fifty million years ago, London would have had a hot, tropical climate and be covered with marshy swamps full of crocodiles, turtles, and hippopotamuses.

❏ The Sahara desert was covered with ice 450 million years ago. About 5,000 years ago, the Sahara was covered in grass and trees. Cave paintings found in the Sahara show that lions, buffalos, and elephants roamed the area in earlier times.

❏ A million years ago, the world's air temperature averaged 95°F (35°C).

❏ Only 200,000 years of the last 2 million have been warm interglacial periods.

❏ An ice core 1,200ft (366m) long can show what the climate was like 1,400 years ago.

❏ Climatic change may have killed off the dinosaurs 65 million years ago. There have been many explanations put forward for the sudden disappearance of the great reptiles which roamed the Earth for over 140 million years. One theory supposes that the climate suddenly became colder and the cold-blooded dinosaurs could not adapt to the new conditions. Perhaps a huge meteor struck the Earth, spreading a layer of dust throughout the atmosphere, blocking out the Sun's light and heat.

The ice ages

For billions of years, the Earth's climate has followed the same regular pattern: long cold ice ages, lasting millions of years, followed by short warmer periods. In an ice age, the temperature fluctuates. There are cold periods, called glacials, and warmer periods called interglacials. We are lucky. Although we are living in an ice age, the last glacial period ended about 10,000 years ago. We are living in a warm interglacial period. During the last glacial period, ice spread over much of the Earth's surface. In North America, glaciers reached as far south as the Great Lakes. Icebergs floated on all the world's oceans. Today, the ice of Greenland and Antarctica is left over from these times; some of it is 3 million years old. The permanent ice on the Arctic is younger, a mere 700,000 years old. The succession of glacial and interglacial periods happens because of changes in the Earth's orbit. Every 90,000 years, the Earth's orbit becomes stretched by the gravitational pull of the other planets. This also causes the tilt of the Earth to change gradually, making the Earth wobble as it goes around the Sun. These variations cause the amount of radiation reaching the Earth from the Sun to alter, and so affect the Earth's climate.

Mammoths had long curved tusks which they used to clear away snow and dig up plants to eat.

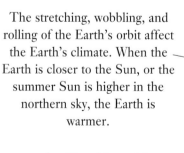

The stretching, wobbling, and rolling of the Earth's orbit affect the Earth's climate. When the Earth is closer to the Sun, or the summer Sun is higher in the northern sky, the Earth is warmer.

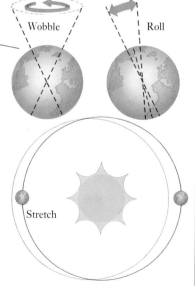

Wobble

Roll

Stretch

Woolly mammoths were a kind of elephant which roamed the northern hemisphere during the last glacial period.

One of our early relatives was Neanderthal Man who lived in Europe until 35,000 years ago. Their short compact bodies helped keep out the cold.

Mammoths were covered in long hair, and a thick layer of fat to help keep warm. Many frozen mammoths have been dug up in Siberia.

❑ We are living today in the Quaternary ice age that began about 3 million years ago. There have been about 35 cold glacial periods and 35 warm interglacial periods during that time.

The extent of the ice sheet 18,000 years ago

❑ During the last glacial period, which started about 70,000 years ago and ended 10,000 years ago, one-third of the Earth was covered with ice 800ft (244m) thick.

❑ Ice ages are caused by the continents gradually changing their positions over millions of years. If the continents drift toward the poles, then ice and snow can form and lie on the ground for long periods. If the continents lie in the tropics, snow and ice does not form at the poles.

❑ Ice age conditions can be found today in the Arctic and Antarctic. Temperatures in the Arctic can vary between 32°F and −40°F (0°C and −40°C). The average temperature in the Antarctic is −46°F (−51°C).

Mount Liotard, Antarctica. Conditions in the Antarctic today are like those of the last glacial period when ice sheets covered much of the Earth.

When ice spread across much of the northern hemisphere animals such as the Polar bear could wander from continent to continent.

The little ice age

The period between about 1400 and 1850 is called the Little Ice Age. During this time, the temperature was about 4-7°F (2-4°C) lower than it is today. There were many very cold winters. The River Thames that flows through London was frequently frozen over. In 1607, the first of many 'frost fairs' was held on the Thames, when a city of tents, including swings, sideshows, food stalls, and taverns were built on the ice. The greatest frost fair was held in 1683 when the ice was 10in (26cm) thick and the river was frozen for two months. The last frost fair was held in 1813 when the ice was thick enough for an elephant to be driven across the frozen river, attracting a great crowd. The river has not been frozen since. The cause of the Little Ice Age, and other similar short-term climate changes, is difficult to find.

Perhaps the Sun shone less brightly during the cold periods. There is some evidence that when the Sun has few sunspots, the climate is colder. Perhaps at these times, the churning cauldron of the Sun is less active, producing both fewer sunspots and less radiation to warm the Earth. Scientists also suspect that volcanic activity can affect climate. When a large volcano explodes, much dust is thrown into the atmosphere. The dust could cloak the ground from the Sun's rays, producing cold weather.

The number of sunspots (yellow) changes gradually over a period of years. Sunspot activity seems to be related to the Earth's climate.

The eruption of Augustine volcano, Alaska, in 1986. The ash cloud rose 38,000ft (11,500m) into the atmosphere.

The bitterly cold winter of 1812-13 forced Napoleon's troops to retreat from Russia.

This photograph was taken shortly after the end of the Gulf War of 1991. Many oil wells in Kuwait were left on fire. The smoke obscured the Sun, producing cold weather.

In 1683-4 there was frost in London from November to April and the Thames froze over.

❑ In the winter of 1431, every river in Germany froze over.

❑ In 1492, the year that Columbus sailed for America, the northern seas were covered with ice. The Pope complained that no bishop had been able to visit the Viking colony in Greenland for 80 years. He did not know that the colony had been wiped out by the cold in 1450, more than 40 years earlier.

❑ During the winter of 1564-5, Queen Elizabeth I of England strolled across the frozen River Thames in London.

❑ Ice skating was first introduced to England in 1662 when King Charles II watched a demonstration of the sport on the frozen River Thames.

❑ Napoleon's retreat from Moscow in 1812 was hampered by the harsh winter weather, typical of that of the Little Ice Age. The bitter winter took a terrible toll of Napoleon's army: of the 450,000-strong force, only 40,000 returned alive.

❑ Dust from the eruption of the volcanic island of Krakatoa in Indonesia in 1883 remained in the atmosphere for two years, and caused unusually red sunsets around the world for six months.

The greenhouse effect

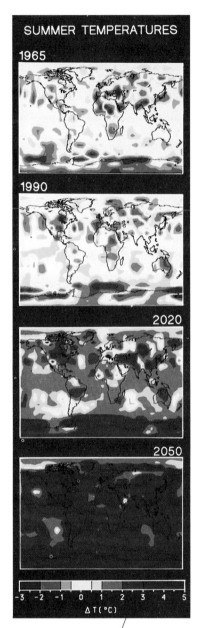

SUMMARY TEMPERATURES

1965

1990

2020

2050

-3 -2 -1 0 1 2 3 4 5
Δ T (°C)

Projected changes in temperature up until the year 2050 made by the NASA Goddard Institute for Space Studies. Red and orange areas indicate increased temperatures. This prediction assumes that the emission of greenhouse gases will continue to increase at current rates.

The world is getting warmer. Throughout the 1980s, weather stations around the world reported rising temperatures. There are fluctuations, with some years hotter than others, but a pattern of gradually increasing temperature is clear. Many people think that the temperature increases of recent years are due to a buildup of 'greenhouse gases' in the atmosphere. Greenhouse gases act in the same way as the panes of glass in a greenhouse: they let heat in but prevent the outflow of heat. As greenhouse gases build up in the atmosphere, so the theory goes, more and more heat is trapped in the atmosphere and the world becomes warmer. The main greenhouse gas is carbon dioxide, which is produced when fossil fuels, such as oil and coal, are burnt. The amount of carbon dioxide in the atmosphere has been increasing since the 1880s as the result of the increasing use of these fuels. Burning the tropical rain forests to clear the land is also releasing vast quantities of carbon dioxide each year. Another greenhouse gas is methane, which is produced by rotting plants and by animals. The amount of methane in the atmosphere, though small, is increasing. Chlorofluorocarbons or CFC's are also greenhouse gases. They are 20,000 times more efficient than carbon dioxide at trapping heat. CFC's are used in refrigerators and aerosols. In the late 1980s, CFC's in the atmosphere were increasing rapidly and their use was restricted.

Carbon dioxide, the main greenhouse gas. Solid, freezing carbon dioxide, called dry ice, in the jar is vaporizing to form a mist of water droplets. The carbon dioxide is invisible.

Huge clouds above the cooling towers of a coal-burning power station. As well as water vapor, power stations give off carbon dioxide, boosting global warming. The stations also emit sulfur dioxide, which causes acid rain.

The Maldive Islands in the Indian Ocean are in danger of being submerged if the level of the sea rises. If the world's ice sheets melt, the level of the seas would rise by an estimated 225ft (70m). Coastal cities such as New York and London would be flooded.

An artist's impression of the surface of Venus, a planet with an atmosphere of almost pure carbon dioxide. The planet suffers from a run-away greenhouse effect, with a surface temperature of around 900°F (480°C). The balloon is carrying a space probe.

FACT FILE

❑ If the amount of carbon dioxide in the atmosphere was doubled, the average temperature of the Earth would rise by 4°F (2°C). Many forecasters expect atmospheric carbon dioxide to double by the year 2025, if steps are not taken to reduce fossil fuel consumption. The world would then be warmer than at any time in the last 100,000 years.

❑ About 5,500 million tons (5,000 million tonnes) of carbon in the form of fossil fuel is burned each year. This releases 110,000 million tons (100,000 million tonnes) of carbon dioxide into the atmosphere.

❑ Cars produce about four times their own weight in carbon dioxide each year. The average home produces 50 tons (45 tonnes) of carbon dioxide each year.

❑ Burning a 100 watt light bulb for an hour using electricity generated from fossil fuel results in the release of 0.1 kilogram of carbon dioxide into the atmosphere.

❑ If there were no greenhouse gases in the atmosphere, the average temperature on Earth would be 5°F (−15°C), instead of the present average of 57°F (14°C).

Looking ahead – future weather

Satellite image of the Atlantic Ocean, showing the distribution of plankton in the water. Plankton absorb carbon dioxide from the atmosphere and help reduce the greenhouse effect.

Wind farm producing electricity at San Gorgonia Pass, near Palm Springs, California. The search for renewable sources of energy must be continued if global warming is not to worsen.

What will the weather be like in the future? Let us gaze into a crystal ball that science provides. It is clear that our weather and climate are very changeable. However, it seems that cold weather is more often experienced than the warm weather that the world has enjoyed since around 1850. Ice ages are much more common than warm periods. Furthermore, another ice age is due soon, perhaps within the next 1,000 years. So perhaps we should expect the Earth's climate to become colder over the next few centuries. However, the opposite seems to be the case. The world is becoming warmer because we are burning more fossil fuels. We are also destroying the tropical rainforests that absorb carbon dioxide. As a result, carbon dioxide, and other greenhouse gases, are building up in the atmosphere, increasing the greenhouse effect. If this trend were to continue, we could be in for a very hot time. Future weather will be the result of a tug-of-war between these opposite trends: the trend toward the colder weather that seems to be normal for our planet, and the trend toward warmer weather that human activity seems to be producing. Which trend will win? It is not easy to predict the future, but it is clear that human activity must be carefully controlled if we are not to tip the balance toward a much hotter climate.

Solar energy. At Barstow, California, an array of 1,818 mirrors focus sunlight onto a steam generator.

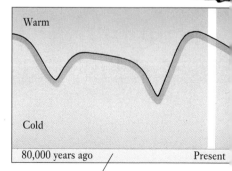

Warm

Cold

80,000 years ago   Present

The predicted variation of average summer temperature for the next 120,000 years, assuming that the greenhouse effect is controlled.

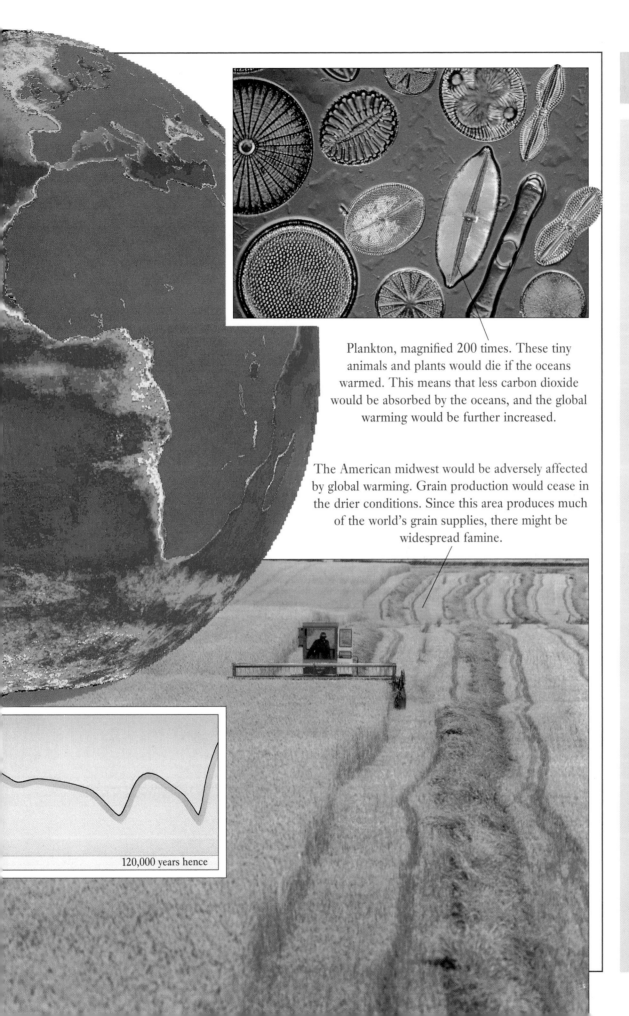

Plankton, magnified 200 times. These tiny animals and plants would die if the oceans warmed. This means that less carbon dioxide would be absorbed by the oceans, and the global warming would be further increased.

The American midwest would be adversely affected by global warming. Grain production would cease in the drier conditions. Since this area produces much of the world's grain supplies, there might be widespread famine.

120,000 years hence

❏ We rely on the Sun's output remaining steady for our climate to support life on Earth. If the Sun's energy output dropped by one-tenth, the entire Earth would be covered in ice one mile (1.6km) thick; if the Sun's energy increased by 30 percent, all life on Earth would be burnt to a cinder.

❏ If today's ice caps melted completely, sea level would rise across the world by between 200 and 230ft (60 and 70m). This means the Statue of Liberty would be immersed up to her armpits, and the clock face on the Houses of Parliament in London would be under water.

❏ Every three seconds an area of South American rain forest the size of a football field is cut down.

❏ About 110,000 million tons (100,000 million tonnes) of carbon dioxide enter the atmosphere each year as the result of burning fossil fuels. To remove this amount of carbon dioxide from the atmosphere requires a forested area the size of Australia.

❏ In the future, satellite technology will play an even more important part in our lives. New Earth resources satellites planned for the 1990s will be able to measure wind speeds, sea temperature, and humidity with much greater accuracy, and so help refine our model of the world's climate.

Chill factor

Moving air or wind has a cooling effect on a body exposed to it. When the wind blows at 20mph (32km/h) and the air temperature is 34°F (1°C), we feel as cold as we would on a calm day with a temperature of −38°F (−39°C).

Fish shower

In 1859 a shower of fish fell from the sky in Glamorgan, Wales. The fish covered an area the size of three tennis courts.

Airborne water

A large cumulonimbus cloud can hold enough water for 500,000 baths. Most of the water droplets in a cloud re-evaporate and never reach the ground; only one-fifth actually falls as rain.

Highest waterspout

In 1898 a waterspout off the coast of Australia reached a height of 5,013ft (1,528m), the highest on record. It was about 10ft (3m) across.

Lucky geese ▲

In 1978 a flock of geese flying across Norfolk, England, were caught in the updraft of a tornado and later dropped out of the clouds in a line stretching for 28 miles (45km).

Long, hot summers

Temperature and crime are correlated. Many more crimes are committed in the hot summer months than in the cold winter months.

Energetic Sun

The Sun's energy production each second is enough to supply the electrical needs of the U.S.A. for 50 million years at current rates of consumption.

Falling frogs

In 1939, a shower of tiny frogs fell on the English town of Trowbridge. Strong winds had carried them aloft from streams and ponds.

Converting temperatures

A useful quick way roughly to convert temperatures from Celsius to Fahrenheit is to double the Celsius and add 30; for example 12°C=24+30=54°F.

Mirage across the sea

In 1798, a mirage of the French coast was seen from Hastings, a town in southern England, 60 miles (100km) away. A hundred-mile (160km) stretch of the French coast from Calais to Dieppe was seen clearly for three hours.

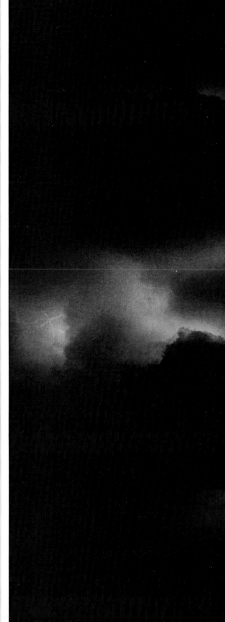

Nights of thunder ▲

In a belt along the equator (between 35°N and 35°S), there are 3,200 thunderstorms each night, some of which can be heard 18 miles (29km) away.

Heavy current

The core of a upward lightning stroke is only a few inches across but can carry a current of 100,000 amperes, enough to run nearly 8,000 electric toasters at the same time.

Lucky man

American Park Ranger Roy Sullivan from Waynesboro in Virginia has survived being hit by lightning seven times. He was first hit in 1942, escaping with the loss of a big toe nail. In 1969, he lost his eyebrows in the same way. In 1970, he was slightly burnt on the left shoulder by lightning. Lightning set his hair on fire in 1972 and 1973. In 1976, he was struck on the ankle, and in 1977 was burnt on the torso.

Lightning strikes many times

Lightning has hit the Empire State Building in New York as frequently as 12 times in 20 minutes. The building is hit by lightning about 500 times a year.

Pennies from heaven

In 1940, silver coins fell from the skies on to the town of Gorky, Russia. A tornado had lifted up an old money chest and dropped the coins it contained as the wind carried it along.

Longest lightning

The longest lightning flashes measured have been 20 miles (32km) in length. Long flashes occur most often in flat country that is covered by high clouds. The smallest flashes may measure less than 300ft (91m).

Exactly equal

Minus 40°C is exactly minus 40°F. This is the only temperature for which the readings on both scales are equal.

Most thunder

The town of Tororo in Uganda had thunder on an average of 251 days each year during the period 1967-76, the highest number on record.

An exciting journey

In 1931 a tornado in Minnesota lifted a train, with 117 passengers aboard, weighing 91 tons (83 tonnes), into the air to a height of 80ft (25m) before dropping it into a ditch.

SUPERFACTS

Not perfect
Paradise, Mt. Ranier, Washington State, is not all it should be. It holds the record for the most snow in one year: 1,224in (31,090mm) fell between February 19, 1971 to February 18, 1972. Paradise has an average annual snow fall of 575in (14,600mm). Hotel walls in Paradise have to be specially strengthened to prevent them being crushed by the weight of snow in winter.

Longest glacier
The longest glacier in the world is the Lambert Glacier in Australian Antarctic Territory. It is up to 40 miles (64km) wide and at least 250 miles (402km) long.

Large iceberg ▶
In 1977 an iceberg 45 miles long and 25 miles wide (72km by 40km) drifted north from Antarctica, threatening to disrupt shipping around Cape Horn. The iceberg was estimated to contain enough water to supply California for 1,000 years.

Wet and dry
In North America, rainfall varies from 1.2in (30mm) each year in Bataques, Mexico, to 266in (6,756mm) at Henderson Lake, British Columbia. In Europe, rainfall varies from 6.5in (165mm) at Astrakhan, Azerbaijan to 185in (4,648mm) at Grkvice, Yugoslavia.

Wettest place
The wettest spot on earth is Mount Waialeale in Hawaii with an average 470in (1,194mm) of rain each year, the height of a three-story building. On average, it rains on 350 days each year.

Worst downpour
The most intense downpour of all time occurred at Barst, Guadeloupe, West Indies, on November 26, 1970, when 1.5in (38mm) fell in 1 minute.

The 30-30-30 rule
To survive in the Artic or Antarctic, explorers must remember that human flesh freezes in 30 seconds when exposed to a 30mph wind at a temperature of −30°F.

Coldest permanently inhabited place
The 4,000 inhabitants of Oymyakon in Siberia have to endure temperatures that may fall as low as −89°F (−67°C), which make it the coldest permanently inhabited place on Earth.

Lowest temperature
The lowest ever temperature was recorded at Vostok, a research base in Antarctica on July 21, 1983: −128.6°F (−89.2°C).

Human warmth
The human body radiates heat. A single person sitting in an unventilated room measuring 1,000 cubic feet (28m^3) raises the temperature by 15°F (8°C) in an hour.

Naked comfort
The most comfortable temperature for an unclothed person is 86°F (30°C). At this temperature the body radiates as much heat as it receives and a balanced temperature results. The most comfortable temperature for a lightly clothed person is 70-75°F (21-24°C).

How far?

The distance of lightning from you can be estimated by measuring the time between the flash being seen and the thunder heard. Sound travels at about 1 mile in 5 seconds (1km in 3 seconds), so the distance to the lightning is found by dividing the time in seconds between the flash being seen and the thunder by 5 (to obtain the distance in miles) or by 3 (to obtain the distance in km).

Snowiest day ▶

The heaviest snow fall for a 24-hour period is 76in (1,930mm) at Silver Lake, Colorado, on April 14-15, 1921.

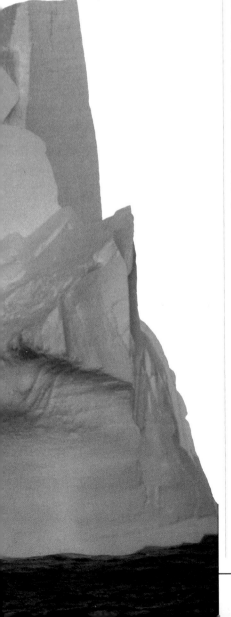

Least variable temperature

Garapan, on Saipan, in the Marianas Islands, Pacific Ocean, has the world's most unvarying temperature. The temperature ranges between 67°F (19°C) and 88°F (31°C), a differential of only 21°F (12°C).

Most variable temperature

The world's most variable temperatures occur at Verkhoyansk in Siberia, eastern Russia. The temperature swings between −94°F (−70°C) and 98°F (37°C).

Electric fire

Static electricity sometimes causes a bright bluish green glow around the top of a ship's mast, or the wings of an aircraft. The glow is called 'St. Elmo's fire' after a 4th-century bishop from Italy.

Most rapid temperature rise

The most rapid temperature change recorded occurred at Spearfish, South Dakota, at 7.30 on the morning of January 22,1943. The temperature rose by 49°F (27°C) in two minutes, from −4°F (−20°C) to 45°F (7°C).

Hottest place

The hottest temperature in the shade was recorded at al'Azīzīyah, in Libya, on September 13, 1922: 136.4°F (58°C).

Most sunshine ▼

The town of Yuma in Arizona, has over 4,000 hours of sunshine a year on average, making it the sunniest place on Earth.

Under water

An inch of rain falling over a square mile would deliver water weighing about 64,700 tons (25mm over an area of one square km weighs about 25,000 tonnes).

Heaviest snow fall

The heaviest ever snow storm occurred on February 13-19, 1959 at Mt. Shasta Ski Bowl, California, during which 189in (4,800mm) of snow fell.

Coldest average temperature

The place with the coldest average temperature is Polus Nedostupnosti (Pole of Cold), Antarctica, with an average temperature of −72°F (−58°C).

Most changeable day

On January 23-24, 1916, at Browning, Montana, the temperature fell by 100°F (56°C) in one day, from 44°F (7°C) to −56°F (−49°C), the greatest daily change recorded.

Hot spot

162 consecutive days with temperatures above 100°F (38°C) were recorded at Marble Bar, Western Australia, between October 1923 and April 1924. The maximum temperature reached was 121°F (49.4°C).

Wettest day

On March 15-16, 1952, over 73in (1,800mm) of rain fell on Cilaos, Réunion in the Indian Ocean, in 24 hours, the greatest sustained downpour recorded.

GLOSSARY

Acid rain
Rain which is acidic due to dissolved sulfur dioxide and other pollution. Rain in industrial areas can be as acidic as lemon juice.

Anticyclone
A region where the atmospheric pressure is higher than in surrounding areas. Often called a 'high.' Winds blow outward from anticyclones.

Atmosphere
The layer of air which surrounds the Earth. Air consists of four-fifths nitrogen and one-fifth oxygen, with small amounts of other gases and water vapor. The atmosphere is divided into layers: the troposphere at the bottom, and above it the stratosphere, mesosphere, and thermosphere.

Atmospheric pressure
The pressure exerted by the atmosphere, usually measured in millibars. At sea level, the average pressure is 1,013 millibars.

Aurora borealis
Also called the 'northern lights,' the lights seen in the night sky in northern latitudes. The equivalent display in the southern hemisphere is called the 'aurora australis.' They are caused by particles from the Sun colliding with the upper atmosphere.

Barometer
An instrument that measures atmospheric pressure. Falling pressure usually means that storms are coming. Rising pressure means fine weather.

Beaufort scale
A scale used to measure the speed of the wind in a series of numbers, from 1 to 12. Each number corresponds to easily observable effects, such as tree movements.

Carbon dioxide
A gas found in small amounts in the atmosphere. It has no color or smell. Too much carbon dioxide in the atmosphere – the result of pollution and the burning of fossil fuels – causes global warming.

CFC
Abbreviation for chlorofluorocarbons, chemicals that pollute the atmosphere, damaging the ozone layer.

Cirrus cloud
Wispy white clouds that occur high in the atmosphere. They are made of ice crystals blown by strong winds.

Cold front
The region where an advancing mass of cold air meets a stationary mass of warm air. The cold air makes the warm air rise, and clouds form.

Condensation ▷
The process whereby a gas changes into a liquid by cooling. For instance, water vapor condenses to form rain droplets.

Convection current
A current of hot liquid or gas that flows from a hot place to a colder one. Liquid or gas rises when it is heated; cold liquid or gas sinks. The two flows set up a continuous current.

Cumulus cloud
Fluffy-looking clouds with rounded tops like a cauliflower. Cumulus clouds form during fine weather, but they can develop into storm clouds, called cumulonimbus.

Cyclone
An area of low atmospheric pressure, also called a depression. Violent tropical storms in the Indian Ocean are also called cyclones.

Depression
See cyclone

Dew point
The temperature below which water vapor condenses into water. If the temperature falls below the dew point during the night, dew will form on the grass.

Evaporation
The process by which a liquid slowly changes into a vapor, through the effect of heat or air currents. A wet object dries if left in the warm because the water contained in it finally evaporates.

Front ◁
The region between two different air masses. There are three types of front, warm, cold, and occluded, all of which bring rain.

Geostationary satellite

A satellite which always stays above the same point on the Earth's equator. Many of these satellites are used for weather observations. The satellite seems to be stationary in the sky, at a height of 22,300 miles (35,900km), because its orbital speed matches the speed of the Earth's own rotation.

Greenhouse effect

The warming of the Earth's atmosphere caused by gases, called greenhouse gases, which prevent heat from escaping from the Earth into space. Carbon dioxide is the main greenhouse gas.

Hadley cell

The circular currents of air immediately north and south of the equator. Hot air rises at the equator, flows away at high altitude, sinks at the Tropics and flows back to the equator at low level.

High

An area of high atmospheric pressure, creating stable weather. See anticyclone.

Humidity

The amount of water that is contained in the air. When the humidity is high, the weather is muggy and uncomfortable. Relative humidity is the humidity expressed as a percentage of the maximum possible.

Infrared radiation

Heat rays. Radiation that carries heat. Infrared radiation has a wavelength just longer than that of red light. Infrared radiation can pass through mist and clouds and is often used to take satellite photographs.

Isobar

A line on a weather chart which joins places at which the sea level air pressure is the same. The closer the isobars are together, the stronger the winds will be blowing.

Latent heat

The heat that is absorbed or emitted when a liquid changes to a vapor or vice versa. Latent heat is called 'hidden heat' because it is absorbed or emitted without causing a temperature change.

Low

An area of low atmospheric pressure. See cyclone.

Meteorology

The science that studies the weather. It provides the information used to make weather forecasts.

Millibar

The unit in which atmospheric pressure is measured. The average pressure of the atmosphere is 1,013 millibars.

Occluded front

The region where a moving mass of cold air overtakes a mass of moving warm air. The warm air is lifted up and clouds form.

Ozone layer

A layer in the upper atmosphere where the gas ozone is concentrated. The ozone layer shields us from the harmful effects of ultraviolet radiation from the Sun.

Precipitation

Water that falls to the ground from the clouds. Depending on the temperature, precipitation can be in the form of rain, sleet, hail, dew, or snow.

Radiation ▲

Energy that can travel through empty space, in the form of waves, called electromagnetic waves. Light, X-rays, infrared, and ultraviolet rays are all forms of radiation.

Refraction

The way that a ray of light is bent when it passes at an angle from one transparent substance to another. For instance, refraction causes a spoon dipped in a glass of water to appear bent.

Relative humidity

The amount of water in the air, expressed as a percentage of the maximum possible. When the air can hold no more water, the relative humidity is 100 percent.

Spectrum

The rainbow-colored band of light seen when white light is split by being passed through a prism. Each color corresponds to a wave of different wavelength; red is the longest wave and violet the shortest.

Stratus cloud

Low-level clouds which form layers. Stratus clouds may bring drizzle or possibly light coverings of snow.

Synoptic weather chart

A weather chart drawn using observations which are all made at the same time. Weather charts in newspapers are synoptic charts.

Ultraviolet radiation

Invisible rays which occur naturally in sunlight. Ultraviolet radiation has a wavelength just shorter than that of violet light. Ultraviolet radiation causes our skins to tan.

Warm front

The region where an advancing mass of warm air meets a stationary mass of cold air. The warm air rises above the cold air, and clouds form.

Water cycle

The circulation of water in nature. Water evaporates from the seas, lakes, and rivers into the atmosphere to form clouds. Rain falls from the clouds and flows off the land to return to the seas, lakes, and rivers.

Page numbers in **bold** type indicate major references including accompanying photographs. Page numbers in *italics* indicate captions to illustrations.

Two different types of weather 'power' in action. Brilliant lightning flashes serve as a backdrop to a wind farm near Barstow, California. The turbines harness the power of the wind to generate electricity.

The publishers wish to thank the following photographers and agencies
who have supplied photographs for this book. The photographs have
been credited by page number and position on the page: (B) Bottom,
(T) Top, (C) Center, (BL) Bottom Left, etc.

Colorific!:
Jim Argo Picture Group: 85(TR), 85(B)
John Hawkins: 79(T)
John Moss: 72
Roswell Angier Picture Group: 38
St. Petersburg Times: 76(T)

Mary Evans Picture Library: 48(T), 49(C), 70(L,
   Lawrence Saint), 85(TL), 94-95(T), 95(B)

Eric & David Hosking: 50, 60-61, 75(TL)

Frank Lane Picture Agency:
Phil Carol: 22
K. Ghani: 92-93(T)
Tony Hamblin: 18(BR)
H. Hautala: 25(T)
David Hoadley: 42-43
H. Hoflinger: 43(T)
Daphne Kinzler: 100
R.P. Lawrence: 81(T)
P. and A. Lewis: 14(C)
S. McCutcheon: 39, 59(T), 62, 77(TL)
NASA: 31
Mark Newman: 32(T), 93(B)
Maurice Nimmo: Front endpaper, 64(T)
Philip Perry: 66-67
A.A. Riley: 28(T)
R. Steinau: 43(B)
Bob Stone: 74-75
John Tinning: 42(T)
R. Van Nostrand: 11(TR)
L. West: 60(BR)
Roger Wilmshurst: 11(BC)
W. Wisniewski: 13(T)

McDonnell Douglas Corporation: 53(T), 58(T)

The Meteorological Office, Bracknell:
S.D. Burt: 83(CR)
S. Cornford: 54(T)
Crown Copyright: 41(T), 55(T), 55(B), 56, 82-
   83(T), 83(B), 84
J.F.P. Galvin: 82
Keith Herrington: 87(BR)
F.D. Oltmanns: 75(C)
G.A. Robinson: 83(TR)
The State University of New York: 47(C)
U.S.A.F.: 66(TR)

NASA: 12(T), 19

Science Photo Library:
Agema Infrared Systems: 14(B)
Doug Allen: 79(B), 102-103
Alex Bartel: 23(CL), 85(CL)
Julian Baum: 80(B)
Ken Biggs: 105
Martin Bond: 62-63(B), 68(B)
Brian Brake: 71(CL)
Dr. Jeremy Burgess: 11(BL), 83(CL), 104(CR)
E.H. Cook: 103(B)
Tony Craddock: Back endpaper
Earth Satellite Corporation: 71(CR), 86-87,
   94(BR)
ESA: 34-35, 41(BL), 87(T)
Fred Espenak: 10-11
Graham Ewens: 42(B)
Dr. Brian Eyden: 35(T)
Dan Farber: 44(B)
Malcolm Fielding, Johnson Matthey plc: 27(C)
Richard Folwell: 96(CR)
Simon Fraser: 23(CR), 60(BL), 65(T), 90(B),
   91(TR), 92-93(B)
Gordon Garradd: 38-39, 64(B)
David Hardy: 17(T), 97(BR)
Adam Hart-Davis: 68(T), 78
John Heseltine: 90(TL)
Jan Hinsch: 99(T)
John Howard: 80(T)
Arthur Johnson, U.S. Library of Congress: 17(C)
Dr. David Jones: 28(BL)
Phil Jude: Half-title page, 26-27, 27(B)
Keith Kent: 64-65, 80-81, 100-101
Stephen Krasemann: 12(B)
R.E. Litchfield: 90-91(T)
Lawrence Livermore Laboratory: 16
Dr. R. Legeckis: 51(C), 73(C)
Will McIntyre: 68-69
John Mead: 20-21(B), 65(B), 73(B), 76-77
Peter Menzel: 21(TR), 32-33, 37, 40-41, 58-59,
   59(B), 95(T), 98(T), 98(B)
Lawrence Migdale: 41(BR)
Hank Morgan: 89(BL)
NASA: 15, 17(B), 18-19, 44-45, 45(T), 46, 52-
   53(T), 56-57, 58(B), 67(TL), 67(TR), 69, 86
NASA, Goddard Institute for Space Studies:
   88(B), 96(L)
NASA, GSFC: Title page, 47(T, Hasler and
   Pierce), 48-49, 51(B), 98-99 (Dr. Gene Feldman)
National Center for Atmospheric Research: 75(TR)
NOAA: 45(B), 47(B, John Wells), 53(C)
NOAA/NESDIS: 8
Claude Nuridsany and Marie Perennou: 76(B),
   77(TR), 78-79, 79(C), 103(T)

Omikron: 13(C)
David Parker: 27(T), 35(B), 89(BR)
Joe Pasieka: 61(L)
Steve Percival: 62-63(T)
Philippe Plailly: 12-13, 88(TL)
Dr. Morley Read: 61(C), 72-73
John Reader: 93(T)
Roger Ressmeyer, Starlight: 10
Gregory Sams: 88-89
Robin Scagell: 34(T)
SPL: 16-17, 52, 94(L)
Sinclair Stammers: 71(T)
Sheila Terry: 96-97
Alexander Tsiaras: 81(B)
Jonathan Watts: 30-31
Williams & Metcalf: 33
Kent Wood: 14-15
P. Woiceshyn, JPL: 49(T)
World View/S. Rezvani: 21(C)

Silvestris/Frank Lane Picture Agency:
Albinger: 24-25 (four oval pictures)
A.N.T.: 34(B)
Nils Bahnsen: 52-53(B)
Walter Geiersperger: 75(TC)
Kozeny Günter: 32(B)
Erich Huber: 36
Janicek: 66(BL)
Rainer Kiedrowski: 104(B)
Boris Kornetzky: 90-91(B)
Josef Lughofer: 29(B)
Hans-Peter Merten: 70-71
Burkhard Monker: 26
Dietmar Nill: 60(T)
Monika Rapkre: 20-21(T)
Ingo Riepl: 50-51
Norbert Rosing: 28(BR), 29(T)
Horst Schäfer: 68(CL)
Bruno Schug: 97(T)
Martin Wendler: 48(B)

The Telegraph Colour Library:
C. Bonington: 18(BL)
Robert Coultas: 57(T)
F. Dalgety: 57(B)
M. Goddard: 53(B)
Frank Lane Agency: 43(C)
NASA: 55(C)
SF N.R.S.C.: 22-23, 54-55
Space Frontiers: 63
Telegraph Colour Library: 99(B)
V.C.L.: 30, 87(BC)

Red sky at night – tomorrow should be fine.